REVISE AQA GCSE (9–1) Geography

REVISION WORKBOOK

Series Consultant: Harry Smith

Author: Rob Bircher

Also available to support your revision:

Revise GCSE Study Skills Guide   9781447967071

The **Revise GCSE Study Skills Guide** is full of tried-and-trusted hints and tips for how to learn more effectively. It gives you techniques to help you achieve your best – throughout your GCSE studies and beyond!

Revise GCSE Revision Planner   9781447967828

The **Revise GCSE Revision Planner** helps you to plan and organise your time, step-by-step, throughout your GCSE revision. Use this book and wall chart to mastermind your revision.

For the full range of Pearson revision titles across KS2, KS3, GCSE, Functional Skills, AS/A Level and BTEC visit:
www.pearsonschools.co.uk/revise

Contents

• •

AQA publishes Sample Assessment Material and the Specification on its website. This is the official content and this book should be used in conjunction with it. The questions have been written to help you practise every topic in the book. Remember: the real exam questions may not look like this.

3
4

Natural hazards

1   Which **one** of the following provides the best definition
of a natural hazard?

> Some multiple-choice questions ask for **one** answer, some for **two**. Make sure you check before answering.

A   An event that has threatened life and property ☐

B   A disaster in a natural area with a low human population ☐

C   A natural event that has directly caused the deaths of 100 people or more ☐

D   A natural event that has directly caused any people to be injured or killed ☑   **(1 mark)**

2   Study **Figure 1**, a photograph showing a volcano evacuation route sign near
Mount Rainier, Washington state, USA.

Figure 1

State what type of hazard is featured
in **Figure 1**.

> Remember that there are three main types of natural hazard: tectonic, biological and weather.

Tectonic

(1 mark)

Guided   3   Outline **one** reason why the risk of the hazard indicated in **Figure 1** would be
increased if there was significant population growth in the area around
Mount Rainier.

If the human population significantly increased this could increase

congestion on the roads along the evacuation routes. This would

increase the risk of the hazard because evacuation

could take longer, there are more

people would be in danger of being

exposed to the natural hazard   **(2 marks)**

$\frac{4}{5}$

Plate tectonics theory

1 Study **Figure 1**, a cross section showing the structure of the Earth.

Figure 1

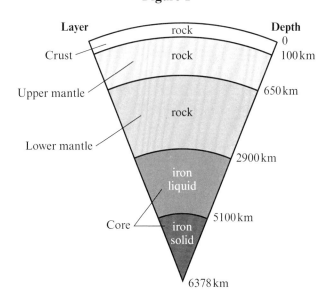

What is the thickest layer in the cross section of the Earth?

A   Crust   ☐

B   Upper mantle ☐

C   Lower mantle ☐

D   Core   ☑   **(1 mark)**

⟩ **Guided** ⟩ 2 State **one** difference between oceanic and continental crust.

Continental crust is normally made of ......less.... dense... ^rock.......... whereas

Oceanic crust is more dense. However continental crusts are thicker.   **(2 marks)**

3 Outline how **convection currents** are connected to plate tectonics theory.

> **Outline** means you have to describe the main features of something and give some development.
> Don't waste time explaining or examining here.

Convection currents in the Mantle underneath the crust make the plates move.   **(2 marks)**

Plate margin processes

1 Study **Figure 1**, a map showing the distribution of volcanoes around the world.

Figure 1

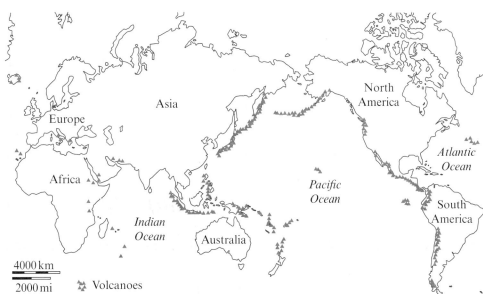

4000 km
2000 mi   ▲▲ Volcanoes

Describe the distribution of volcanoes
in **Figure 1**.

> Make sure you know the meaning of **distribution** – the
> way something is spread out over a geographic area.

Volcanoes are most commonly found
around the plate boundaries close to
the pacific ocean.

(2 marks)

2 Describe the physical processes taking place at **one**
type of plate margin.

> Remember that there are three main
> types of plate margin: constructive,
> destructive and conservative.

Type of plate margin: Destructive Margin

The oceanic plate (pacific) subducts
under the continental plate (south
America) then a volcano is created.

1

(2 marks)

> **Guided**

3 Explain why earthquakes are often associated with **destructive** plate margins.

Destructive plate margins are where oceanic and continental plates

meet and the oceanic plate subducts under the continental one. The

collision of the plates ..... causes pressure to build

up and tremors to occur. However,

Magma is released.

2

(4 marks)

9/12

 Named examples # Tectonic hazards: effects

> Guided

1 Outline what is meant by the term **primary effects** of a tectonic hazard.

> When you are asked to outline the meaning of a term, you just need to provide a **definition** of that term.

Primary effects are things that happen ....in response to...... a tectonic hazard. For example, rescuing people injured by collapsed buildings

(2 marks)

2 Outline the secondary effects of **one** named tectonic hazard on property and people.

> A tectonic hazard can be an earthquake or a volcanic eruption. Remember that a tsunami is a secondary effect of a tectonic hazard, so a tsunami example as a secondary effect would be appropriate here.

Name of tectonic hazard: ......Nepal Earthquake 2015......

The Nepal earthquake 2015 had a magnitude of 7.8. It's secondary effects included the avalance on Mount Everest killing 19 people. More than 1 million people were left homeless and repairing inorastruct. was expensive.

③

(4 marks)

3 Using named examples, describe and explain the primary effects of tectonic hazards in **two** areas of contrasting levels of wealth.

> For this question, you need to both **describe** and **explain** the primary effects of the two tectonic hazards.

Name of first tectonic hazard: ......L'Aquila, Italy 2009......

Name of second tectonic hazard: ......Kashmir, Pakistan 2005......

There were 79700 More deaths by collapsed buildings in Kashmir. This could be because of the lack of earthquake resistant (or strong) infrastructure than in Italy. This also meant thousands of people were injured. Around 3 million people were left homeless after the earthquake in Kashmir but only 60,000 in L'Aquila. Again this could be because of the amount of poor quality buildings but also because of a more dense population in Kashmir. This meant more people lost their homes.

④

(6 marks)

7/9

 Named examples # Tectonic hazards: responses

1 Study **Figure 1**, a table showing data about earthquakes in 2010.

Figure 1

Location of earthquake	Magnitude on Richter scale	Number of deaths
Haiti	7.0	160 000
Qinghai, China	6.9	2698
Maule Region, Chile	8.8	521
Sumatra, Indonesia	7.7	435
Papua, Indonesia	7.0	17

(a) From **Figure 1**, which earthquake had the greatest magnitude?

Maule Region, Chile

(1 mark)

(b) Using **Figure 1**, compare the number of earthquake deaths with earthquake magnitude.

Haiti had the most deaths as a result of an earthquake probably because it is an LIC. whereas Papua in Indonesia had only 17 deaths and Sumatra had 435.

(2 marks)

Guided

(c) Suggest **two** reasons why the earthquake with the greatest magnitude did not cause the most deaths.

Reason 1: If the earthquake happened in an area with very low numbers of people living there, that would help explain why the earthquake with the greatest magnitude did not have the highest number of deaths.

Reason 2: Prediction and evacuation is poor due to the inability to afford for this and aid.

(2 marks)

(d) The number of deaths caused by tectonic hazards is usually much higher in poorer areas than in wealthier areas. Outline why problems with immediate responses can help explain this.

> Although the question does not specifically ask for named examples, you can still use examples if you like.

The number of deaths is much higher in poorer countries such as Haiti because they can't afford high quality treatments for injured people and the disease risk is increased due to lack of clean water (cholera). In wealthier countries they can afford this as well as good, drink and shelter for evacuated people.

(4 marks)

5

Had a go ☐ Nearly there ☐ Nailed it! ☑

8/8

Living with tectonic hazards

1 Study **Figure 1**, which shows one of the benefits of living in areas close to tectonic activity.

Figure 1

> Look carefully at the picture. This benefit relates to accessing geothermal activity to help deal with the impacts of a cold winter climate.

Identify the benefit shown in **Figure 1**. ...Geothermal energy.... **(1 mark)**
Providing heat.

2 Study **Figure 2**, a map showing population density around Mount Tambora in the Asia-Pacific region.

Figure 2

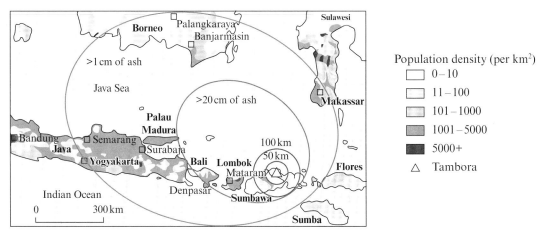

> **Guided**

(a) Describe the population density shown in **Figure 2**. Use data in your answer.

It is clear to see that the population density is unevenly distributed.
Population is more dense in Makassar,
Matarami (Lombok) and Palau Madura which
all have approximate densities of 1001-5000 Per km².
Regions that are 50 -100Km away **(4 marks)**
from Mount Tambora are sparsely populated with
(b) Explain why people would still choose to live close to the volcano. 0-10 km²
They May not want to leave due to geographical
inertia and because they have to find new
employment. Also, Many tourists are attracted **(3 marks)**
to these areas and people who are employed
in tourism would benefit. Soil is fertile and
full of minerals due to volcanic ash which attracts farm

$\dfrac{7}{8}$

Tectonic hazards: reducing risks

1 There are many instruments used to predict when tectonic hazards will occur. Which **one** of the following does a seismometer measure?

  A   The amount of sulphur dioxide given off   ☐

  B   The temperature of the magma   ☐

  C   The shaking of the ground (earthquakes)   ☑

  D   The ash emitted by the volcano   ☐   **(1 mark)**

2 Outline **two** methods used to predict when a volcano is likely to erupt.

> Make sure you know which instruments can be used to help predict volcanic eruptions.

Method 1: Tiltmeters measure changes in the slopes (shape) of a volcano.

Method 2: Magma bulges can be monitored and measured for where magma collects and thermometers to check its temperature. **(4 marks)**

> **Guided**

3 Study **Figure 1**, an infrared satellite image of a volcano in Alaska, USA.

Figure 1

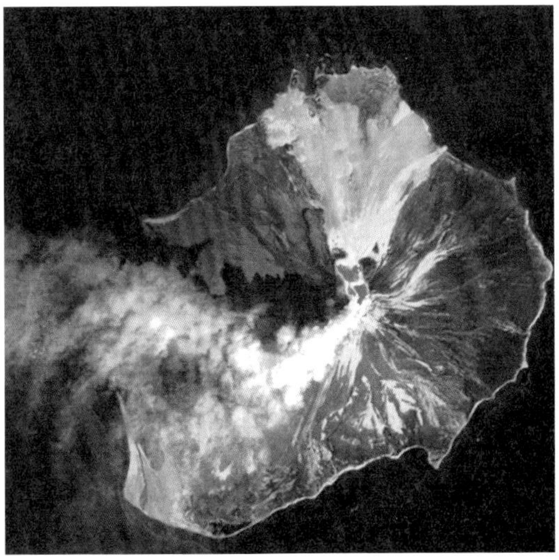

Explain how satellite images could be used to predict a potential volcanic eruption.

> Remember that a satellite is a platform orbiting the Earth with instruments that can take images of the Earth's surface.

Satellite images use infrared which measures surface temperatures around the volcano. If an increase in temperature is detected, an eruption can be predicted.

(3 marks)

②

Weather hazards

Global atmospheric circulation

4/6

1 Study **Figure 1**, which shows a model of global atmospheric circulation with the annotations missing.

Figure 1

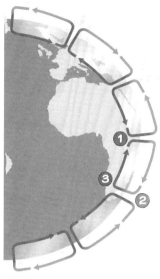

Which **two** of the following would be the best annotations to add?

A At **1**: Warm air rises at the Equator, creating low pressure ☑

B At **1**: Warm air rises at the Equator, creating high pressure ☐

C At **2**: Cool air falls at around 30° north and south of the Equator ☑

D At **2**: Cool air falls, creating low pressure ☐

E At **3**: Warm air rises at around 30° north and south of the Equator ☐

F At **3**: Warm air rises, creating high pressure ☐   **(2 marks)**

2 Complete this statement.

> Read the whole sentence carefully as it will give you clues about the best words to choose to fill the gaps.

Apart from moving from belts of high pressure to ....low pressure.........., surface winds are also affected

by the Earth's ....atmosphere......, which gives surface winds a curved path. ① **(2 marks)**

⟩ Guided ⟩ 3 The Sun's heat energy is most intense at the Equator. Explain **one** way in which this heat energy is transferred away from the Equator towards the poles.

One way that heat is transferred is through the atmospheric circulation

cells. ......is when warm air from the equator

rises to create low pressure.................................

.... **(2 marks)** ①

8

$\dfrac{4}{7}$

Tropical storms: distribution

1 Study **Figure 1**, a map showing the global distribution of tropical storms.

Figure 1

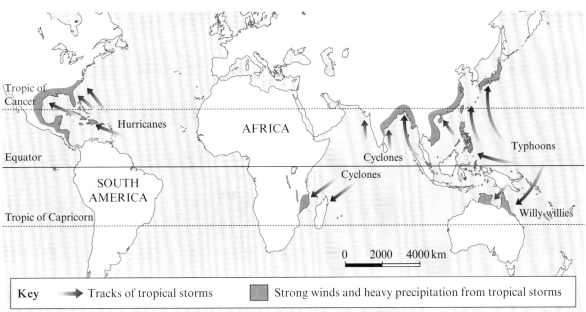

Outline what is meant by the track of a tropical storm.

The direction in which the tropical storm travels until it reaches land. **(1 mark)**

Guided

2 Describe and explain the distribution of tropical storms shown in **Figure 1**.

> You need to use your own knowledge of the global distribution of tropical storms to explain the distribution you see, rather than spending a lot of time describing what the map shows.

The map shows the tropical storms being largely restricted to the tropics. There are three main reasons for this location.

First, these storms are powered by warm ocean temperatures – the seawater needs to be above 26.5°C and these temperatures are only found in late summer and autumn in the tropics.

Second, *Most tropical storms occur between 5° and 30° North and South of the equator where the water temperatures stay high.*

③

(6 marks)

Continue your answer on your own paper. You should aim to write about half a side of A4.

9

5/6

Tropical storms: causes and structure

1 Study **Figure 1**, a diagram of a cross section through a tropical storm.

Figure 1

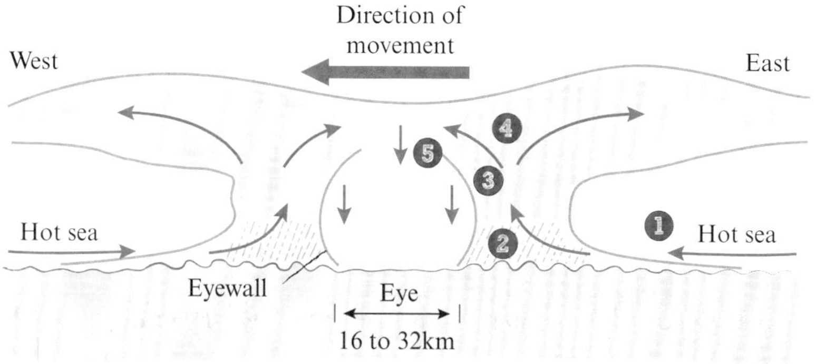

The eyewall surrounds the eye. Here the air is rapidly spiralling upwards and there are high winds and torrential rain.

The eye is the centre of the storm. Here there is falling air, light winds and no rain.

(a) The numbers on **Figure 1** relate to five stages in the development of a tropical storm. These stages have been provided below, out of order. Identify the correct numbers for the three missing stages.

> Make sure you study the diagram carefully for extra information that can help you select the correct answers.

1 Warm, moist air rises and condenses, releasing huge amounts of energy, powering the storm.

2 As the air rises up, it sucks in more warm, moist air behind it.

☐5☐ In the centre of the storm, air falls, forming the eye.

☐4☐ The air condenses as it rises and cools, forming huge clouds and heavy rain.

☐3☐ The air spirals up rapidly which causes high winds.

(2 marks)

Guided

(b) **Figure 1** shows that warm sea temperatures are required for tropical storms to form. Suggest **two** other factors that are important if tropical storms are to form.

Factor 1: High humidity is important because ....large amounts.... of moisture form in the air making it rise so that it condenses soon afterwards.

Factor 2: Pre-existing low pressure disturbances are important because ...Surface winds are increased and this means that warm moist air is rising.

③

(4 marks)

6/8

Tropical storms: changes

1 Which **one** of the following is used to measure the magnitude of a tropical storm?

    A   The Richter scale   ☐

    B   The Beaufort scale   ☑

    C   The Saffir-Simpson scale   ☐

    D   The Mercalli scale   ☐   **(1 mark)**

Guided

2 Study **Figure 1**, a table showing data about climate and fatalities for two recent tropical storms.

Figure 1

Tropical cyclone	Location	Highest wind speed	Height of storm surge	Pressure (mb)	Fatalities
Typhoon Haiyan, November 2013	Philippines	315 km/h	4.23 m	895	6340
Hurricane Sandy, October 2012	USA	185 km/h	5.20 m	940	149

Using the information from **Figure 1**, compare the magnitudes of Typhoon Haiyan and Hurricane Sandy.

Wind speed is one of the main ways in which tropical storms are measured

and compared with each other. Typhoon Haiyan's highest wind speed was

130 km/h faster than Hurricane Sandy. This means that .....there......

were very strong winds and a more

damaging tropical storm was created

which led to 6191 more fatalities

than Hurricane Sandy. In addition to this,

Typhoon Haiyan had a lower pressure

than Hurricane Sandy and tropical   ③   **(4 marks)**

storms form better in lower pressures.

3 Explain how climate change could affect the intensity and distribution of tropical storms.

> Think about the impact of climate change on ocean temperatures as well as atmospheric changes.

More oceans will stay above

27°c for longer periods of time

and so more areas will experience

tropical storms. This is because

climate change will make temperatures

higher and storms will be more intense,

and more damage will be created.   ③   **(4 marks)**

🌐 Named example Tropical storms: effects

$\frac{8}{10}$

> **Guided**

1 Outline **two** primary effects associated with tropical storms.

Tropical storms can bring extreme weather conditions such as strong winds,

storm surges and high rainfall.
storm surges are rises in sea level
due to low pressure and high winds.

① **(2 marks)**

2 Explain **one** reason why tropical storms present a particular danger to low-lying coastlines.

Storm surges can occur on a large
scale. These surges are large rises in
sea level due to low pressure and
high winds.

(2 marks)

3 Describe and explain the secondary effects of a tropical storm that you have studied.

> Remember that secondary effects are the longer-term impacts that happen as a result of the primary effects: for example, landslides caused by heavy rain, homelessness caused by storm surge damage, or loss of income due to coastal flooding of farmland or tourist resorts.

Name of tropical storm: Hurricane Katrina, Mississippi + Louisiana
2005. Hurricane Katrina made hundreds
of thousands of people homeless due to
the number of houses destroyed by
flooding. In addition to this, 230,000
jobs were lost from businesses being
damaged or destroyed and water
supplies were polluted with sewage and
chemicals from overflown sewages
and aiding the spread of disease.
The total cost of the damage was
estimated at $150 billion.

⑤ **(6 marks)**

Weather hazards

$\dfrac{4}{4}$ 🌐 Named example **Tropical storms: responses**

1   Study **Figure 1**, a photograph showing people waiting for evacuation from flooding caused by Hurricane Katrina in New Orleans, USA, 2005.

Figure 1

(a) Complete this statement.

Apart from rescuing people left in danger by the primary or secondary effects of a tropical storm, one other immediate response to a tropical storm is

collecting bodies to prevent the spread of disease.   **(1 mark)**

Guided

(b) Suggest **one** challenge for the emergency services in rescuing the people shown in **Figure 1**.

The flooded streets would make it very difficult for road vehicles to

reach this location, so rescue attempts should happen by boat or via helicopter.

(1 mark)

2   Outline **two** long-term responses that could be used to protect the people shown in this picture from the effects of future tropical storms.

> You do not need to know the specific long-term responses to Hurricane Katrina in order to answer this question. Instead, use your knowledge of long-term responses to make two general suggestions.

Response 1: Build houses on stilts and make buildings hurricane resistant

Response 2: Improve flood defences such as levees and flood gates.

(2 marks)

5/5

Tropical storms: reducing risks

1 Study **Figure 1**, which shows a portable radar apparatus (a doppler on wheels, or DOW) recording data from an approaching hurricane in Florida, USA.

Figure 1

(a) Which **one** of the following can radar provide to help predict the likely impacts of tropical storms when they make landfall?

    A The speed at which a tropical storm is moving ☐

    B The track taken by the tropical storm over the previous hours and days ☑

    C Precipitation data – likely rainfall levels ☐

    D Forecasting of the likely track once the tropical storm has made landfall ☐ **(1 mark)**

⟩ **Guided** ⟩

(b) Suggest **two** ways in which monitoring can help reduce the effects of tropical storms.

> Remember that monitoring is closely linked to forecasting (prediction).

First way: Scientists can analyse the data produced by monitoring the tropical storm and find out useful information, such as what local factors intensify tropical storms. This can help planning and protection measures.

Second way: Monitoring the storm can prepare local people to evacuate and install further house protection methods such as window shutters.

(4 marks)

UK: weather hazards

1 Study **Figure 1**, a table showing UK weather records.

Figure 1

Record type	Record	Location and date
Highest daily maximum temperature	38.5°C	Faversham, England, 10 August 2003
Lowest daily minimum temperature	−27.2°C	Altnaharra, Scotland, 30 December 1995
Highest 24-hour rainfall total	279 mm	Martinstown, England, 18 July 1955
Highest 2-day rainfall total	405 mm	Thirlmere, England, 4–5 December 2015

Source: Met Office, UK Climate

(a) Martinstown is in Dorset. The average yearly rainfall for Dorset is 770 mm.
What percentage of Dorset's average yearly rainfall is 279 mm? Give your
answer to one decimal point.

.............36.2 %.. **(1 mark)**

(b) Suggest **one** possible hazard from a very high daily
maximum temperature.

....Heatwave - Deaths due........
to heat exhaustion Heatstroke.

> Remember that a (natural) hazard
> is a natural event that is a threat to
> people and to property.

(1 mark)

(c) Suggest **one** possible hazard from a very low daily
minimum temperature.

....Snow and ice - deaths due....
to the cold, hypothermia, Influenza.

> For this question, think of the
> weather conditions that would be
> produced by very low temperatures
> and the threats that this could
> pose to both people (e.g. health-
> related) and property (e.g. damage
> to property).

(1 mark)

Guided

(d) Explain **two** possible hazards that could occur as a result of very high
24-hour or two-day rainfall totals.

Hazard 1: River flooding – both long duration and high intensity rainfall
can result in rivers exceeding their carrying capacity and flooding
populated areas along their banks.

Hazard 2: Damages infrastructure due to
flooding and economic loss due to
the closure of businesses.

.... **(4 marks)**

Ec
So ten

 **Example** # UK: extreme weather

1   Study **Figure 1**, an extract from a newspaper report on the York floods in 2015.

Figure 1

York floods bring misery to hundreds of residents

The floods that hit York on Boxing Day 2015 caused extensive damage to 600 homes. Hundreds of residents had to be rescued during the night as river waters rose rapidly following the wettest December on record. Residents began cleaning the mud and sewage-contaminated water out of their homes, then began the long process of drying out their houses to make them habitable again. The national cost of the floods is estimated at £5 billion, with £1 billion of the total coming from residents and business owners who did not have insurance or found out after the flood that their insurance would not cover all the damage that had been done. Some families, unable to pay for the repairs their houses needed, have even become homeless.

Businesses were also badly affected, with pubs, shops, offices and factories unable to open for months after the floods. This meant their owners lost a lot of money. For those working in tourism, there were worries that people would not come to York because of concerns that flooding might happen there again.

Assess the extent to which the economic impacts of extreme weather effects are more significant than the social or environmental impacts. Use **Figure 1** and an example you have studied.

> **SPaG** stands for spelling, punctuation and grammar. Good SPaG means being accurate with your spelling and punctuation all the way through your answer, using correct grammar to help ensure your answer is easy to understand, and using a wide range of specialist terms in an appropriate way.

....

....

....

....

....

....

....

....

....

....

....

....

....

....

(9 marks + 3 marks for SPaG)

> Continue your answer on your own paper. You should aim to write about one side of A4.

UK: more extreme weather

1 Study **Figure 1** and **Figure 2**, maps showing average maximum temperature and rainfall for the UK in 2015. The maps show how far the temperature and rainfall were above or below a long-term average for the period 1961–1990.

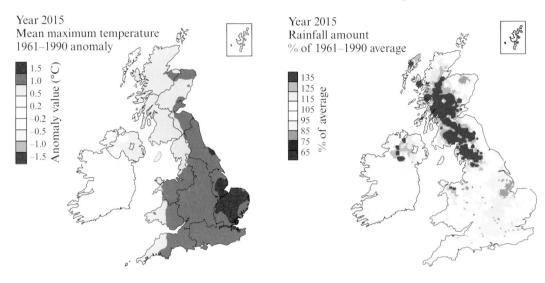

Figure 1

Year 2015
Mean maximum temperature
1961–1990 anomaly

Anomaly value (°C)
1.5
1.0
0.5
0.2
–0.2
–0.5
–1.0
–1.5

Figure 2

Year 2015
Rainfall amount
% of 1961–1990 average

% of average
135
125
115
105
95
85
75
65

(a) Which **two** of the following statements about **Figure 1** and **Figure 2** are correct?

   A Everywhere in the UK experienced rainfall amounts in 2015 that were above the long-term average for 1961–1990. ☐

   B Everywhere in the UK experienced mean average temperatures that were above the long-term average for 1961–1990. ☐

   C The parts of England that experienced the highest above-average mean maximum temperatures also included an area that experienced 75–85 per cent less rainfall than the long-term average for 1961–1990. ☐

   D The parts of Scotland that experienced the highest above-average rainfall amounts also had mean maximum temperatures that were no higher than the long-term average for 1961–1990. ☐   **(2 marks)**

> **Guided**

(b) 'Weather is becoming more extreme in the UK.'
Use evidence to support this statement.

> Your answer should make two more developed points, using evidence from the maps to support them.

Extreme weather can be defined as weather that is

significantly different from average weather conditions.

The temperature map (Figure 1) provides good evidence of 2015 being

extreme because nowhere in the UK recorded average temperatures

that were the same as or below the long-term average for 1961–1990.

Some parts of the UK were 1.5°C warmer on average than ....

....

.... **(6 marks)**

Continue your answer on your own paper. You should aim to write about half a side of A4.

$\frac{4}{7}$ # Climate change: evidence

1   Study **Figure 1,** a graph showing data on carbon dioxide (CO_2) concentrations recovered from ice cores from an Antarctic ice sheet for the period since the last Ice Age until 9000 years ago. The CO_2 concentrations are recorded as parts per million by volume (ppmv).

Figure 1

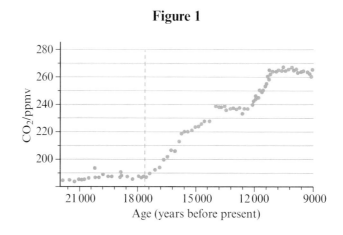

(a)   Ice cores can extend up to 3 km in length and, for the oldest ice sheet layers, can go back 800 000 years. Which **one** of the following locations would you expect to have the oldest, deepest ice sheets?

    A   Mount Kilimanjaro, Tanzania   ☐

    B   Siachen Glacier, Karakoram mountains   ☐

    C   Iceland   ☐

    D   Antarctica   ☑✓   **(1 mark)**

> **Guided**

(b)   Describe and explain the evidence for past climate change shown in **Figure 1**.

> Remember to show what you know. For example, what are the gases associated with climate change?

Figure 1 shows that atmospheric concentrations of

CO_2 changed significantly from the end of the last Ice Age until 9000 years

ago. At the end of the last Ice Age, 21 000 years ago, CO_2 levels were below

200 ppmv which is very low. However

18 000 years ago CO₂ levels steadily

began to rise reaching over 220ppmv

in the next 3000 years (15,000 years

ago). This meant the climate had gotten

significantly warmer because of the

increase of the greenhouse gas, carbon

dioxide. This gradual rise stopped up until

12,000 years ago where it increased to

260 ppmv before staying constant 9000 years   **(6 marks)**

ago.

③

8/9

Climate change: possible causes

Guided

1   (a)   Explain **two** natural causes of past climate change.

> For this question you need to **explain**, which means give a reason why something occurred. Note the question is asking for **natural** causes.

Reason 1: The amount of heat the Earth receives from the Sun varies because of changes to the orbital cycle, which could trigger ice ages.

Reason 2: The Sun's solar output varies from short periods as 11 years to longer periods of hundreds of years meaning sometimes more energy is given.

(4 marks)

(b)   Burning coal in power stations is thought to contribute to the **enhanced greenhouse effect**: global warming produced almost entirely as a result of human factors.

> Remember that human factors that can cause climate change include the use of fossil fuels, agriculture and deforestation.

Explain **two** other types of human activity that are thought to contribute to the enhanced greenhouse effect.

Deforestation contributes to the enhanced greenhouse effect because plants remove carbon dioxide (a greenhouse gas) from the atmosphere to photosynthesise. Also during cement production, limestone which contains carbon is used to form cement. When it is produced CO_2 is released into the atmosphere.

(4 marks)

2   Study **Figure 1**, which illustrates the increase of carbon dioxide (CO_2) in the Earth's atmosphere.

Figure 1

Calculate how much higher the current level of carbon dioxide is than the level in 1950.

400 ppm − 315 ppm = 85 ppm

(1 mark)

$\frac{5}{9}$

Climate change: effects

1 Study **Figure 1**, a cartoon showing potential impacts of climate change.

> For questions like this, make sure you answer the question rather than just describing the picture.

Figure 1

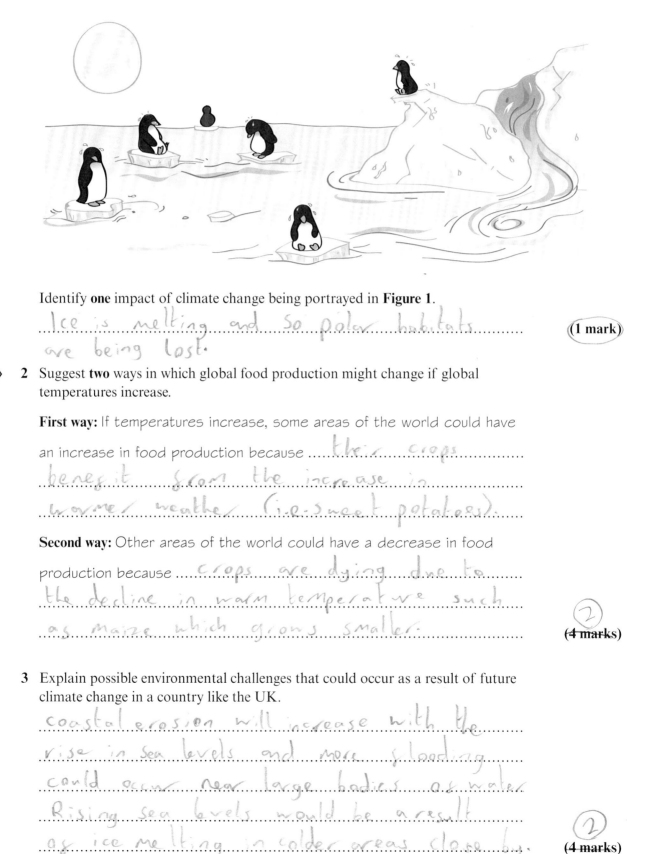

Identify **one** impact of climate change being portrayed in **Figure 1**.

Ice is melting and so polar habitats are being lost.

(1 mark)

Guided **2** Suggest **two** ways in which global food production might change if global temperatures increase.

First way: If temperatures increase, some areas of the world could have an increase in food production because their crops benefit from the increase in warmer weather (i.e. sweet potatoes).

Second way: Other areas of the world could have a decrease in food production because crops are dying due to the decline in warm temperature such as maize which grows smaller.

②

(4 marks)

3 Explain possible environmental challenges that could occur as a result of future climate change in a country like the UK.

coastal erosion will increase with the rise in sea levels and more flooding could occur near large bodies of water. Rising sea levels would be a result as ice melting in colder areas close by.

②

(4 marks)

Mitigating climate change

6/6

1 China has planted 66 billion trees in its dry northern provinces since 1978. Most were planted by hand but increasingly by using aerial reforestation – dropping saplings from the air in special capsules, as shown in **Figure 1**.

Figure 1

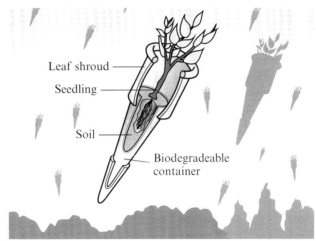

Leaf shroud
Seedling
Soil
Biodegradeable container

(a) Identify **one** advantage of aerial reforestation over planting trees by hand.

Less time is taken to evenly distribute each plant by hand. More planted in less time. **(1 mark)**

(b) China originally began its tree-planting programme to try to reduce desertification, but the programme has since become an important climate change mitigation strategy.

What is meant by the term **mitigation**?

To reduce or prevent the effects of climate change. **(1 mark)**

> **Guided**

(c) China's billions of new trees have been an important part of an increase in the Earth's vegetation. Since 2003, the amount of carbon stored in above-ground biomass has increased by 4 billion tons.

Explain how increasing biomass through tree-planting schemes can help reduce the causes of climate change.

Carbon dioxide (CO_2) is a greenhouse gas, and the increasing CO_2 levels in the atmosphere linked to human activity are a major cause of climate change. Trees and other vegetation pull (CO_2) from the air through photosynthesis and they store it in their leaves, roots or trunks. This means that global temperature is not further increased. More trees means more carbon dioxide is effectively extracted from the atmosphere. **(4 marks)**

21

Had a go ☐   Nearly there ☑   Nailed it! ☐

4/7

Adapting to climate change

1   South East Water manages water supply in the south east of England. In 2015, it completed a Climate Change Adaptation Report, which identified likely impacts of climate change for it's operations. These are shown in **Figure 1**.

Figure 1

- Reduction in surface water availability
- Reduction in groundwater availability
- Increasing demand in warmer weather
- Increased land runoff
- Increase in risk of fluvial flooding

- Increase in risk of groundwater flooding
- Increase in risk of surface water flooding
- Increase in leakage/burst frequency
- Increase in outages from bad weather affecting assets and power supply

(a)   Suggest **one** reason why South East Water might experience increased demand in warmer weather.

Farmers will need more water for their crops.   **(1 mark)**

> **Guided**

(b)   Identify **one** way that South East Water could help its customers to reduce the amount of water they use in their homes.

The amount of water a toilet uses when it flushes can be reduced by

installing water meters and recycling waste water   **(1 mark)**

2   (a)   Suggest **one** reason why increased land (surface) runoff might become more common as a result of climate change.

> Remember that rainfall intensity can affect the infiltration capacity of soil.

To stop lots of rainwater going into soil and destroying crops.   **(1 mark)**

> **Guided**

(b)   One method South East Water is considering to reduce the problems of increased land runoff is encouraging farmers not to leave fields bare of vegetation over winter.

Explain **one** reason why this change in agricultural methods could help reduce the problem of increased land runoff in winter.

While the impact of rainfall on bare soil compacts the soil and

increases surface runoff, plant cover intercepts rainwater

Saturating the soil.   ① **(2 marks)**

(c)   Increasing the amount of infiltration of water into the soil during winter could also help South East Water with which **two** of the following?

A   Reducing the number of leaks from water pipes   ☐

B   Increasing groundwater availability   ☑

C   Reducing the risk of surface water flooding   ☐

D   Increasing availability of water to be abstracted from rivers   ☐

E   Reducing possible contamination of groundwater from agricultural fertilisers and pesticides   ☐

F   Increasing the capacity of reservoirs   ☑   ① **(2 marks)**

A small-scale UK ecosystem

Guided 1 Study **Figure 1**, a diagram of a pond ecosystem.

Figure 1

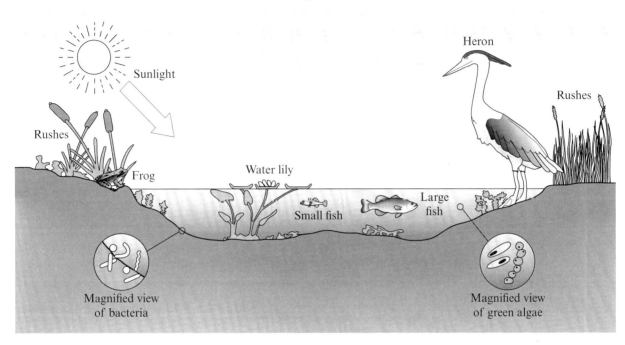

What is meant by the term **ecosystem**?

A community of living organisms (plants and animals) and their physical

environment (sunlight, air, water, rock and soil) which are .....linked.....

to each other and rely on each other.

....

.... **(2 marks)**

2 (a) Use **Figure 1** to identify **one** example for each of the following parts of the pond ecosystem.

> Try not to rush questions like these. It is easy to make a silly mistake.

A producer: .....water Lily.....

A consumer: .....Large fish.....

A decomposer: .....bacteria..... **(3 marks)**

(b) Explain **one** difference between a producer and a consumer in an ecosystem.

A producer converts sunlight energy into food for itself through photosynthesis whereas a consumer has to eat another organism in order to receive energy. **(2 marks)**

$\dfrac{4}{5}$

Ecosystems and change

1 Study **Figure 1**, a diagram of a nutrient cycle for a tropical rainforest ecosystem.

Figure 1

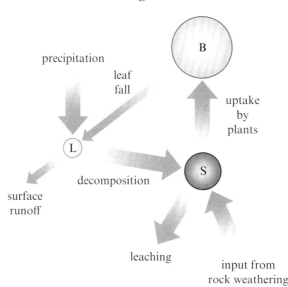

(a) Identify which **one** of the following would be most
    likely to occur in the tropical rainforest ecosystem if
    the input of precipitation into the ecosystem was
    reduced. Use **Figure 1** to help you.

> Work through each option to make
> sure you select the right answer.

   A Increased uptake of nutrients by plants ☐

   B Increased leaching ☐

   C Reduced leaf fall ☐

   D Reduced surface runoff ☑   **(1 mark)**

> **Guided**

(b) Rainforest is often cleared to make way for grazing
    land for cattle. Explain how soil fertility would change
    in this ecosystem if biomass were reduced in this way.

> For this question, you can use
> your understanding of the tropical
> rainforest ecosystem and the
> impacts of deforestation to help
> with your answer.

The biomass store is the largest store in the rainforest ecosystem,

which means that ..... the nutrients is found in the leaf

litter layer. ....

....

....

Heavy precipitation would continue, as would rapid leaching of nutrients

from the soil. As a result, soil fertility would ..... decrease because

..... the nutrients would be transported into

..... rivers instead.   ③

                                                      (4 marks)

$\dfrac{4}{4}$

Global ecosystems

1 Study **Figure 1**, which shows the distribution of large-scale natural ecosystems.

Figure 1

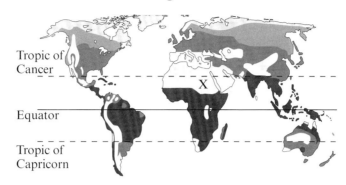

Identify which large scale natural ecosystem is indicated by **X** on **Figure 1**.

A   Tropical rainforest   ☐

B   Temperate ecosystem   ☐

C   Taiga ecosystem   ☐

D   Desert ecosystem   ☑   **(1 mark)**

> **Guided**

2 Describe the global distribution of tropical rainforest.

> When describing global distribution, make sure you state the main areas and refer to **latitude**: how far north or south of the Equator they are.

Tropical rainforests are found .... *North and south of the Equator in South Africa, South America, South East Asia and Australia* .... **(2 marks)**

3 Study **Figure 2**, a climate graph for the taiga large-scale natural ecosystem.

Figure 2

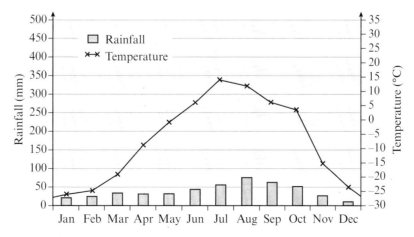

Identify **one** characteristic of the taiga ecosystem from the climate graph shown in **Figure 2**.

.... *Low precipitation* .... **(1 mark)**

$\dfrac{3}{4}$

Rainforest characteristics

1   Study **Figure 1**, a diagram of the different layers within the tropical rainforest ecosystem.

Figure 1

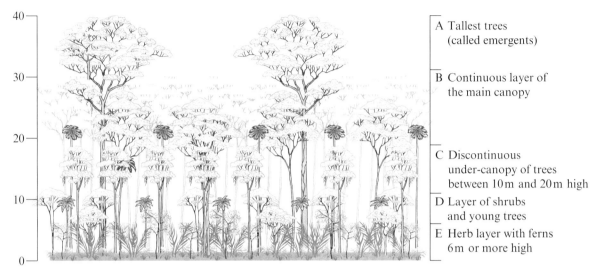

40
30
20
10
0

A Tallest trees
(called emergents)

B Continuous layer of
the main canopy

C Discontinuous
under-canopy of trees
between 10 m and 20 m high

D Layer of shrubs
and young trees

E Herb layer with ferns
6 m or more high

Which **one** of the following strata (layers) of the tropical rainforest is being described?

> This layer is dark, with what little light penetrating through the main canopy then being blocked by the under-canopy. The densely-packed trees mean there is little air movement. The air is extremely humid.

A   Emergent layer ☐   **C**   Under-canopy ☐

B   Main canopy ☐   **D**   Herb layer or forest floor ☑   **(1 mark)**

>**Guided** 2   Plants in the tropical rainforest have warm temperatures (20°C and higher) throughout the year and very frequent, heavy rainfall (rarely under 50 mm a month).

Identify the factor that drives competition between plants and creates the different layers that characterise the tropical rainforest.

Plants compete for ....Sunlight...   **(1 mark)**

3   Complete the labelling on **Figure 2**, showing a profile of a tropical rainforest soil. There are four labels to complete.

> Where some labels are already provided, read these carefully first to help avoid any mistakes.

Figure 2

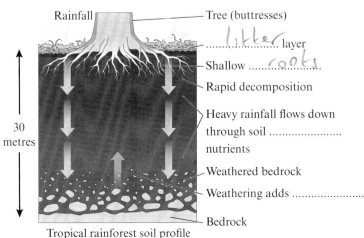

Rainfall   Tree (buttresses)

.........litter........ layer

Shallow .....roots....

Rapid decomposition

Heavy rainfall flows down through soil ....
nutrients

Weathered bedrock

Weathering adds ....

Bedrock

30 metres

Tropical rainforest soil profile   **(2 marks)**

$\dfrac{4}{5}$

Interdependences and adaptations

1 Which **one** of the following is an abiotic component of an ecosystem?

A A tree   ☐

B An insect   ☐

C The soil   ☑

D People   ☐

(1 mark)

> **Guided**

2 Study **Figure 1**, which shows part of the tropical rainforest.

Figure 1

Identify **two** features of the tropical rainforest shown in **Figure 1**.

> **Identify** requires you to **select** and **name**. Don't be tempted to explain the adaptation.

Feature 1: In the centre left of the picture there are buttress roots of a tree.

Feature 2: Leaves have drip tips.

....

(2 marks)

3 Explain **one** way animals have adapted to the tropical rainforest.

Orangutans have long arms to
swing on branches and climb trees.
This helps them to escape from
predators and reach food.

① (2 marks)

Deforestation: causes

6

1 Study **Figure 1**, which shows satellite images of the same area of Brazilian tropical rainforest in 1975, 1992 and 2001.

Figure 1

(a) Describe the changes to the area shown in **Figure 1** from 1975 to 2001.

> Try to use geographical descriptors (such as north, south, east and west) and give approximate amounts of clearance (for example, a rough percentage of the 1975 cover).

In 1975 No deforestation has occured, however by 1992 a small clearance had branched out from South West to North East. Even more so in 2001, roughly 70% of the area has been cleared by deforestation. **(2 marks)**

(b) Causes of deforestation include:

- commercial farming
- subsistence farming
- logging
- mining.

Choose **two** of the causes listed or others that you have studied. Explain how your choices cause deforestation.

> Remember to **explain how** the causes lead to deforestation rather than just describing them.

Cause 1: Subsistence farming ....

....

....

....

Cause 2: ....

....

....

....

(4 marks)

🌐 Case study **Deforestation: impacts**

Guided

1   Outline **one** link between deforestation of the tropical rainforest ecosystem and climate change.

Tropical rainforest biomass acts as a carbon sink – an enormous store

of carbon. Because of this ..... the amount of CO_2 in the atmosphere is reduced. Deforestation destroys the carbon store and so no CO_2 emissions **(2 marks)** are stored and can be released into atmosphere increasing climate change.

2   Outline **one** link between deforestation of the tropical rainforest and increased soil erosion.

> Remember that the soil of a tropical rainforest ecosystem is low in nutrients, while its biomass is a large nutrient store.

Deforestation decreases tropical rainforest biomass containing lots of nutrients. High precipitation causes soil to be eroded at a faster rate as there **(2 marks)** is less plant cover.

3   For a tropical rainforest you have studied, explain how deforestation may impact on that country's economic development.

> You can use your tropical rainforest case study to write about causes of deforestation and also for the impacts of deforestation: economic development, soil erosion and contribution to climate change.

....

....

....

....

....

....

....

....

....

....

....   **(6 marks)**

Rainforest value

Guided 1 Study **Figure 1**, which shows an aerial view of tropical rainforest and the Amazon River, Brazil.

Figure 1

Describe **one** function of a tropical rainforest in terms of regulating the atmosphere.

Trees and plants absorb carbon dioxide from the atmosphere. They therefore

....

....   **(2 marks)**

2 Describe and explain the value of the tropical rainforest for people and the environment.

> Where a question looks at two aspects – here **people** and **the environment** – try to pay equal attention to both aspects in your answer.

....

....

....

....

....

....

....

....

....

....

....   **(6 marks)**

Sustainable management

1 Study **Figure 1**, a graph showing data on the rate of deforestation in the Brazilian Amazon.

Figure 1

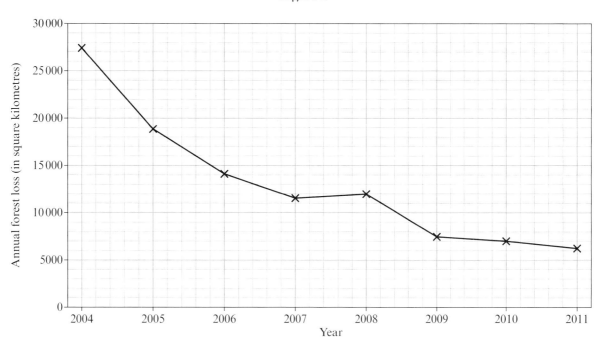

> **Guided**

(a) Describe the trend shown by the deforestation data in **Figure 1**.

The rate of deforestation has declined almost every year between

.... **(1 mark)**

(b) Using your own knowledge of sustainable management of tropical rainforests, suggest **three** reasons for the decline in deforestation rates shown in **Figure 1**.

> Remember that rainforest management includes selective logging and replanting, conservation and education, ecotourism and international agreements and debt reduction.

Reason 1: ....

....

....

Reason 2: ....

....

....

Reason 3: ....

....

.... **(3 marks)**

Hot deserts: characteristics

'Hot deserts' and 'Cold environments' are options: only revise the one you studied.

1 Study **Figure 1**, a map showing the global distribution of hot deserts.

Figure 1

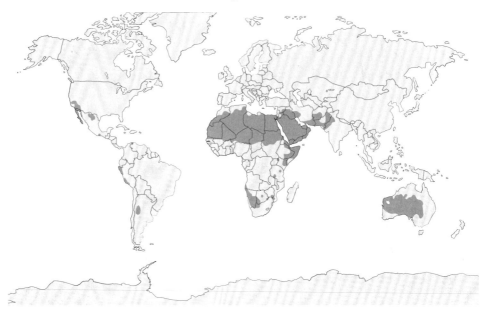

(a) One of the defining characteristics of a desert is low annual precipitation.

Which **one** of the following is the correct definition of
a desert in terms of annual precipitation?

> Make sure you learn key facts like
> this to use in your answers.

A   < 250 mm   ☐

B   > 250 mm   ☐

C   < 25 mm   ☐

D   > 25 mm   ☐   **(1 mark)**

(b) Hot deserts have their greatest extent in north (Saharan) Africa.

State **one** other feature of the global distribution of hot deserts.

.... **(1 mark)**

> **Guided**

(c) Most hot deserts have a very large diurnal range: temperatures into the
    40° or even 50°C range during the daytime, while night-time temperatures
    can drop below freezing. Explain **one** reason why this happens.

The high pressure atmospheric conditions in hot deserts mean that

they usually have clear skies during the day and night, so ....

....

.... **(2 marks)**

The hot desert ecosystem

1   Study **Figure 1**, a diagram showing different plants and animals from a hot desert ecosystem in south-west USA.

Figure 1

> **Guided**

(a)   Using **Figure 1** and your own knowledge, identify and explain **two** plant adaptations that help plants survive in hot desert ecosystems.

> There is a lot of detail in this picture. Looking carefully at it will give you important clues for a good answer.

First plant adaptation: Some plants, like the globemallow, have very deep root systems. These roots can reach down to groundwater a long way beneath the surface.

Second plant adaptation: ....

....

....   **(4 marks)**

(b)   Suggest **two** ways in which desert animals have adapted to the high daytime temperatures of hot desert habitats.

First way: ....

....

Second way: ....

....   **(2 marks)**

Development opportunities

1 Study **Figure 1**, an advertisement for a desert safari in Dubai.

Figure 1

Dubai Desert Safari

Experience the romance and adventure of a 6-hour desert safari. Attractions include:

- racing through the desert in a guide-driven 4x4

- dashing down desert sand dunes in an amazing sandboard experience

- visiting a camel farm and riding a camel

- enjoying a delicious barbeque, cooked under the desert stars

- relaxing to traditional music and belly dancing.

Guided

(a) Identify **one** attraction of hot desert environments for tourists from the UK.

> For questions like this, remember to use the resources you are given – here, the advertisement in **Figure 1**.

A different culture – .... **(1 mark)**

(b) Outline **two** development opportunities in a hot desert environment that you have studied.

> Note that these opportunities do not have to be tourism. Other opportunities include mineral extraction, farming and energy. However, you **do** need to provide relevant case study information.

Development opportunity 1: ....

....

Development opportunity 2: ....

.... **(2 marks)**

(c) 'Hot deserts have excellent potential for energy development.' Use evidence from your case study to support this statement.

....

....

....

.... **(6 marks)**

> Continue your answer on your own paper. You should aim to write about half a side of A4.

⊕ Case study Development challenges

1   Study **Figure 1**, a compound bar graph showing the growth in capacity of all the desalination plants in the world between 2010 and 2016, broken down for the five countries with the largest desalination capacities. Desalination is a process that turns saltwater into freshwater. All five countries featured in the graph have large desert and semi-arid areas.

Figure 1

> Remember to look at the scales and units used on graphs and think about what they mean. Here the unit is m^3/d – cubic metres per day – and 10^6 is 1 million. So the graph measures capacity in millions of cubic metres of fresh water produced by desalination per day.

(a)   According to **Figure 1**, by how much has global desalination capacity increased between 2010 and 2016?

   A   126 million cubic metres per day   ☐

   B   76 million cubic metres per day   ☐

   C   56 million cubic metres per day   ☐

   D   26 million cubic metres per day   ☐   **(1 mark)**

Guided

(b)   Suggest **one** advantage and **one** disadvantage of investing in desalination in order to develop hot desert environments.

> Challenges of developing hot desert environments include extreme temperatures, water supply and inaccessibility. For which challenge does desalination provide a possible solution?

Disadvantage: Desalination is expensive. It requires a large amount of energy to power the desalination process. Solar power can generate some of this energy in hot desert environments, but not all.

Advantage: ....

....

....

....   **(2 marks)**

Desertification: causes

1   Study **Figure 1**, a fact file and a diagram about desertification

Figure 1

Desertification fact file

🔍 2.6 billion people in the world depend on agriculture for their livelihood

🔍 Globally, 52% of agricultural land is affected by soil degradation

🔍 Each year, 12 million hectares of agricultural land are lost due to drought and desertification

🔍 Land degradation affects 1.5 billion people globally

🔍 42% of the poorest people in the world are directly affected by land degradation

Population growth → Increased demand for fuelwood → deforestation → soil erosion

Population growth → Increase in sheep/goats → overgrazing → soil erosion

Population growth → Increase in crop cultivation → overwatering → salinisation

(a)   Which **one** of the following gives the most accurate definition of **desertification**?

   A   The persistent degradation of dryland ecosystems to create desert-like conditions   ☐

   B   The advance of deserts onto farmland   ☐

   C   Unsustainable farming of desert soils   ☐

   D   The formation of a salt layer on top of the soil which makes soil useless for farming   ☐   **(1 mark)**

(b)   Explain **two** ways in which land becomes degraded into desert-like conditions.

> Think about the causes of desertification that you have studied: climate change, population growth, removal of fuelwood, overgrazing, over-cultivation and soil erosion. **Figure 1** also includes salinisation.

First way: ....

....

....

....

Second way: ....

....

....

....   **(4 marks)**

Desertification: reducing the risk

1   Study **Figure 1**, which shows the Fallow Band System for reducing desertification. This system uses 5-metre-wide bands of land between crops. These bands trap soil and reduce soil erosion. The bands are at right angles to the prevailing wind direction. After a year, the bands are used for crops and new bands are left next to them.

Figure 1

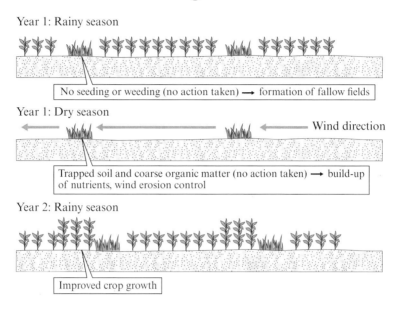

> **Guided**

(a)   Using **Figure 1**, explain **two** ways in which the Fallow Band System could reduce the risk of desertification.

Way 1: One reason for desertification is that over-cultivation of the soil means it loses its organic matter and nutrients, dries up and becomes easily eroded by wind and water. The Fallow Band System helps to keep organic matter and nutrients in the soil because the bands are not used for crops, so they recover nutrients, and the organic matter that grows on them is ploughed back into the soil.

Way 2: Another reason for desertification is wind erosion. The Fallow Band System reduces wind erosion because ....

....

....

.... **(4 marks)**

(b)   Outline **one** reason why the Fallow Band System is an example of appropriate technology.

> Think about why appropriate technology is called 'appropriate' – because it is suited to the needs, knowledge and income of local people and the environment.

....

....

....

.... **(2 marks)**

Cold environments: characteristics

| ‘Cold environments’ and ‘Hot deserts’ are options: only revise the one you studied. |

1   Study **Figure 1**, a climate graph for a cold environment.

Figure 1

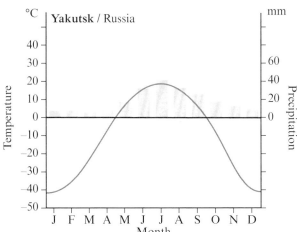

(a) Complete this statement.

Cold environments are environments that experience freezing temperatures

(below ....9.........°C) for long periods of the year.   (**1 mark**)

(b) According to **Figure 1**, for how many months of the year does Yakutsk experience freezing temperatures?

| Remember that precipitation is presented as a bar graph while temperature is presented as a line graph. |

A   Seven months   ☑

B   Five months   ☐

C   Four months   ☐

D   Three months   ☐   (**1 mark**)

Guided

(c) Yakutsk is located in a tundra ecosystem. Identify **two** characteristics of a tundra ecosystem.

Characteristic 1: The main vegetation is low-lying grasses and mosses.

Characteristic 2: ....   (**2 marks**)

(d) Choose **one** of the characteristics from (c) above. Explain how this characteristic is linked to the cold environment of the tundra ecosystem.

....

....   (**2 marks**)

The cold environment ecosystem

1   Study **Figure 1**, which shows a plant called the bearberry growing in Alaska.

Figure 1

Guided

(a)   Suggest **two** ways in which the bearberry is adapted to the physical conditions of cold environments.

> Look carefully at photographs like this. Here you can see that the bearberry grows close to the ground. How might that help it survive the physical conditions of cold environments?

First adaptation: The bearberry has small leaves to minimise water loss in this dry environment.

Second adaptation: Bearberry grows close to the ground so that they don't get blown over and damaged.

(2 marks)

(b)   Cold environments are low-nutrient environments. Complete **Figure 2**, a nutrient-cycle diagram of a cold environment, by labelling the three stores indicated by the circles.

Figure 2

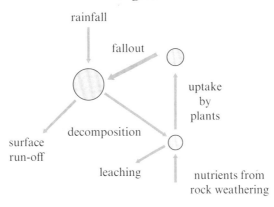

(3 marks)

⊕ Case study Development opportunities

1   Assess the opportunities for development of a cold environment you have studied.

> Think about your case study of a cold environment, which will have covered some or all of the following types of development opportunity: mineral extraction, energy, fishing and tourism.
>
> To assess these opportunities, you need to consider:
>
> • their costs and benefits – for example, the profits that could be made from mineral extraction compared to the costs of working in such a challenging environment, **and/or**
>
> • the obstacles to their development – for example, if international treaties ban or limit some kinds of development in your case study cold environment.

Chosen cold environment: ....

> The exam paper will always give you a space to write the name of your case study location: don't forget to include it!

....

....

....

....

....

....

....

....

....

....

....

....

....

....

....

....

....

....

....

....

.... **(9 marks)**

> Continue your answer on your own paper. You should aim to write about one side of A4.

4/5

Development challenges

1   Study **Figure 1**, a fact file about the Trans-Alaska Pipeline System (TAPS).

Figure 1

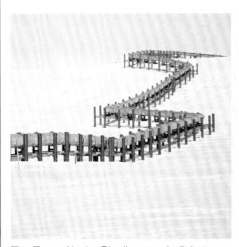

The Trans-Alaska Pipeline was built between 1975 and 1977, following a major global oil crisis. The amount of oil produced in Alaska is declining. By law, once the oil has run out, all trace of the pipeline has to be removed.

Trans-Alaska Pipeline System: fact file

- 800 miles long
- Transports oil from the Prudhoe Bay oilfield to a permanently ice-free port in Valdez, south Alaska
- 420 miles are elevated on 78 000 vertical supports
- There are three separate leak detection systems; controllers can stop the flow of oil within 4 minutes
- 124 000 heat pipes (thermosiphons) transfer heat from the ground to the air to prevent permafrost melting
- The pipeline crosses three mountain ranges and more than 30 major rivers and streams
- 'Pigs' (mechanical devices sent through the pipeline) do most of the maintenance and repair, detecting bending or buckling of the pipeline, and scraping out wax, which precipitates from oil at low temperatures

(a)   Which **two** of the following challenges of developing cold environments explain why the Trans-Alaska Pipeline System uses 'pigs' to scrape wax from the inside of the pipeline?

   A   Extreme low temperature ☑   **C**   Permafrost ☐

   B   Inaccessibility ☑   **D**   High cost of heat and lighting ☐

> **Guided**

(b)   Using your knowledge of the challenges of developing cold environments, suggest **one** reason why 420 miles of the Trans-Alaska Pipeline System is raised up on vertical supports (see **Figure 1**), instead of being buried underground like the other 380 miles of pipeline.

> For this question, think about the challenges posed by the soil in many cold environments.

The pipeline needs to be raised above the ground in areas affected

by permafrost because ......the oil will turn into wax
at low temperatures by the permafrost ① **(2 marks)**
or it could melt and thaw.

(c)   Describe **two** challenges that affect the development of the cold environment that you have studied.

Chosen cold environment: ......Alaska......

Challenge 1: ......Buildings and infrastructure can't
be built directly on the ground. Permafrost will thaw
because of heat produced.

Challenge 2: ......Icy roads make
transportation dangerous and expensive **(3 marks)**

Fragile wilderness

1 Study **Figure 1**, a diagram showing how acid precipitation can damage cold environments that are downwind of industrialised areas.

Figure 1

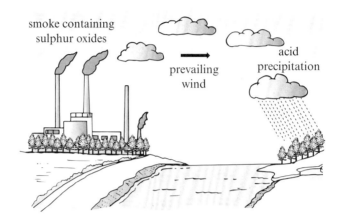

smoke containing sulphur oxides

prevailing wind

acid precipitation

⟩ **Guided** ⟩

(a) Using the information in **Figure 1** and your own knowledge, suggest **one** reason why cold environments are vulnerable to acid precipitation.

Acid precipitation damages plants, kills insect larvae in ponds and

lakes and kills the soil bacteria responsible for decomposition.

Cold environments are vulnerable to this sort of damage because

....

.... **(2 marks)**

(b) 'Climate change is the biggest threat to cold environments.' Use evidence to support this statement.

> You do not need to argue for or against this statement, just **provide evidence** to back it up. Relevant facts and figures from your cold environment case study would be ideal if you have them.

....

....

....

....

....

....

....

....

....

....

....

.... **(6 marks)**

Managing cold environments

1 Study **Figure 1**, which gives information about tourism visits to Penguin Island, Antarctica.

Figure 1

Tourists on Penguin Island, Antarctica

Visiting Penguin Island

Visitor impacts: Footpath erosion, trampling of vegetation, disturbance of wildlife, especially southern giant petrels (seabirds).

Landing restrictions: Ships carrying fewer than 200 visitors. One ship at a time. No more than two ships per day. No more than 100 visitors ashore at any time. No visitors between 10 pm and 2 am.

Behaviour ashore: Walk slowly and carefully. Keep 5 m away from any wildlife and increase this distance if animal behaviour changes. Do not walk on any vegetation.

(a) In 2015–16 (Antarctic spring and summer), 38 478 tourists came to Antarctica. Almost all of the tourists (99 per cent) came by boat.

Of the 38 478 tourists, 79 per cent went ashore in Antarctica. How many tourists was this? Express your answer as a whole number.

> Make sure you know how to convert a percentage into a number where you know the total (100 per cent of the number). You need to divide the total number by 100 to give 1 per cent, then multiply that by the percentage figure (in this case, by 79).

.... **(1 mark)**

 Guided

(b) Using **Figure 1** and your own knowledge of cold environments, describe and explain why tourism to Antarctica is carefully controlled.

> For this question, you need to link ways in which tourism is controlled in Penguin Island with reasons from your own knowledge: for example, trampling of vegetation is controlled because of slow recovery rates in low-nutrient ecosystems.

Visitor numbers are carefully controlled (no

more than 400 people a day, with no visitors

from 10 pm to 2 am) for three main reasons.

It reduces soil erosion ....

....

....

....

....

.... **(6 marks)**

> Continue your answer on your own paper. You should aim to write about half a side of A4.

5/6

Physical landscapes in the UK

1 Study **Figure 1**, a map showing major British rivers.

Figure 1

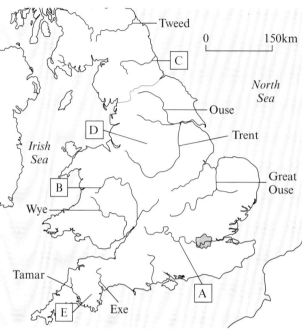

> **Guided**

(a) Write the letters **A**, **B** and **C** into the table below to correctly identify the rivers on the map in **Figure 1**.

A	River Thames
C	River Tyne
B	River Severn

(3 marks)

(b) The following table lists the three longest rivers in the UK. Complete the table below by writing in the name of the third longest river.

> If you are not sure of the answer, look at the map and quickly compare the river lengths by eye. This will give you a chance to get the answer right.

River length	River name
354 km	River Severn
346 km	River Thames
297 km	River Trent

(1 mark)

(c) Two upland areas have been indicated on the map by the letters **D** and **E**. Which upland areas are these?

Upland area D: Pennines

Upland area E: Dorset coast

(2 marks)

Types of wave

Only revise 'Coastal landscapes' if it is one of the options you studied.

1   Waves can be either destructive or constructive. Match the descriptions in the box
    on the right to the correct wave type by placing the description numbers in the correct boxes.

Destructive

2

3

Constructive

1

4

Descriptions

1   Low wave energy
2   Occur in stormy conditions
3   Responsible for erosion
4   Help transport material

(2 marks)

2   Explain the meaning of the term **swash**.

The movement of water at an angle
up the beach.

(1 mark)

3   Complete the following sentences.

Waves hitting the south-west coast of England will have large amounts

of energy because the waves have travelled a long distance. These powerful waves

are destructive, with their ......backwash......

being greater than their ......swash......

(2 marks)

Guided

4   Explain why some waves are more powerful than
    others.

For this question, try to explain **all** the factors
– and include examples, if you can.

The energy of a wave depends on three main factors:

the fetch, the speed of the wind and the length of time the wind has

been blowing. ....

....

....

....

....

....

....

....

(4 marks)

Weathering and mass movement

1 Study **Figure 1**, a newspaper article.

Figure 1

A woman has died after being buried by a cliff collapse in Dorset. Witnesses report that a small landslide was immediately followed by a much larger one which deposited around 400 tonnes of rock and mud from the top of the cliff onto the beach below. The accident happened on a stretch of Dorset's Jurassic Coast, which is composed of soft sandstone. A few days before the accident, Dorset Council had warned visitors to the coast to stay well away from the cliff at all times due to the high risk of landslides and mudflows due to many weeks of heavy rainfall in the area.

(a) Which **one** of the following geographical terms best describes the process which caused this fatal accident? Use a tick to show your answer.

Geographical term	
Weathering	✓
Attrition	
Mass movement	
Saltation	

(1 mark)

>Guided>

(b) Using **Figure 1** and your own knowledge, describe **two** factors that contributed to this landslide.

Factor 1: The wet weather will have saturated the soft sand stone turning it into mud and causing the cliff to fall due to the lack of support

Factor 2: ....

....

....

.... (4 marks)

2 Complete the following sentences.

Freeze–thaw weathering happens when water gets into a crack in a rock. If the temperature falls below 0°C at night, the water

.... and increases in volume, putting pressure on the rock.

> The words you need to add to complete the sentences will be specific. Check that the words you use make sense by reading the completed sentence back to yourself.

Repeated cycles of freezing and thawing weakens the rock, eventually leading to angular pieces of rock breaking away from the cliff and forming a pile at the bottom of the cliff known as ....

(2 marks)

Erosion, transport, deposition

1 (a) Which **one** of the following provides the most accurate description of hydraulic action as a process of coastal erosion?

    A When destructive waves hurl sand and shingle at a cliff, breaking pieces off it   ☐

    B When weak acids in the sea start to dissolve certain types of rock making up the cliff   ☐

    C When wave energy makes rocks and pebbles bump into each other, and break up   ☐

    D When the force of destructive waves pounding the base of cliffs compresses air into cracks in the rocks   ☐ **(1 mark)**

> **Guided**

(b) Identify **two** factors that can increase the rate of erosion on a coast.

First factor: More powerful waves due to stronger winds.

Second factor: ....

.... **(2 marks)**

2 Complete and label **Figure 1**, a diagram to explain the process of longshore drift.

> Complete the diagram to show the way the swash and backwash move material along the beach.

Figure 1

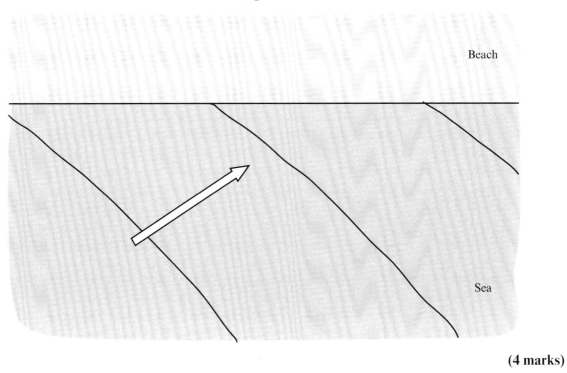

(4 marks)

Erosion landforms

1   Study **Figure 1**, a diagram showing a range of different landforms of coastal erosion.

Figure 1

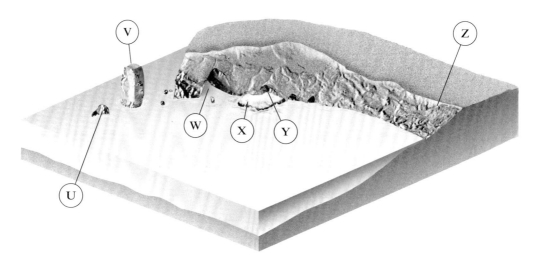

> **Guided**

(a) Complete the following table by writing the letters **U, V, W, X, Y** or **Z** into the boxes to match each landform with the correct label on the diagram.

Landform	Stump	Wave-cut platform	Cliff	Stack	Arch	Wave-cut notch
Letter	U					

(4 marks)

(b) Draw labelled diagram(s) to show how a wave-cut platform is formed.

> Complete your answer by adding one or more diagrams to show the next stages in the formation of this landform.

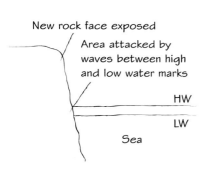

New rock face exposed
Area attacked by waves between high and low water marks
HW
LW
Sea

(4 marks)

Deposition landforms

1   Study **Figure 1**, an Ordnance Survey map extract showing a coastal landform.

Figure 1

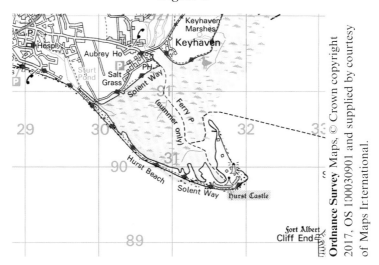

Ordnance Survey Maps. © Crown copyright 2017, OS 100030901 and supplied by courtesy of Maps International.

(a) What type of deposition landform is shown in the map extract in **Figure 1**?

.... **(1 mark)**

Guided

(b) Draw labelled diagram(s) to show why this landform forms.

> Make sure your drawings are clear enough to explain the sequence of formation. It is much more important that the details are clear and accurately labelled than it is to shade or colour in the drawing.

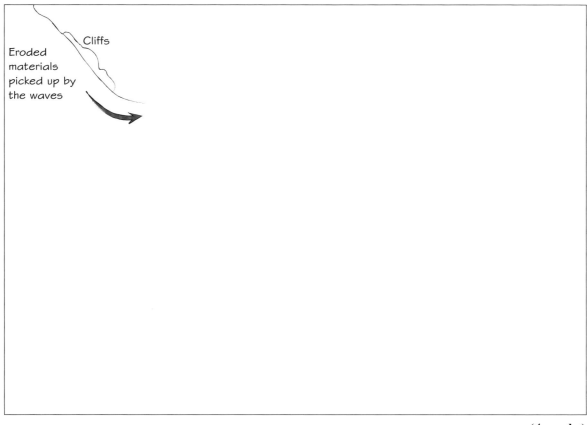

(4 marks)

49

🌐 Named example Coastal landforms

1 Study **Figure 1**, a photograph showing a depositional landform off the coast of Helston, Cornwall.

Figure 1

spit	bar stack
	arch lagoon

What are landforms **A** and **B**? Choose your answers from the box beside the photograph.

A: ....

B: .... **(2 marks)**

2 Study **Figure 2**, a diagram outlining the geology of the Dorset coastline.

Figure 2

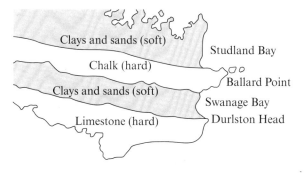

Clays and sands (soft)
Chalk (hard)
Clays and sands (soft)
Limestone (hard)
Studland Bay
Ballard Point
Swanage Bay
Durlston Head

> If you don't know this coastline, don't panic: there are headlands and bays in the diagram so you can write about how those form (on a discordant coastline) and about how headlands erode (caves, arches, stacks…).

Describe and explain the landforms that are likely to form along this coastline.

....

....

....

....

....

....

.... **(6 marks)**

> Continue your answer on your own paper. You should aim to write about half a side of A4.

$\frac{5}{9}$

Hard engineering

1 Study **Figure 1**, a photograph showing an example of coastal defences on the south coast of England.

Figure 1

(a) Name the type of coastal defence shown in **Figure 1**.

Rock Armour

(1 mark)

(b) Describe how the type of coastal defence in **Figure 1** works.

Rock armour is large rocks piled together that trap sediment from the sea to help rebuild the coast.

① (2 marks)

Guided

2 Explain how groynes can help to reduce rates of coastal erosion.

Groynes are used to stop the process of

longshore drift. The sediment gets trapped and

helps build up the beach, which reduces coastal
erosion. less sediment is deposited by
the sea.

Don't just **explain** a groyne. You must link this to how groynes prevent coastal erosion.

② (4 marks)

3 Outline why some places have chosen to use hard engineering coastal defence strategies.

Hard engineering is more efficient
than soft engineering because it
requires less maintenance. they tend to
work better because they inhibit the
natural movement of the sea.

① (2 marks)

Had a go ☐   Nearly there ☑   Nailed it! ☐

$\frac{9}{11}$

Soft engineering and managed retreat

1 (a) Which **one** of the following soft engineering techniques involves removing coastal protection from areas?

    A Beach nourishment ☐   **C** Dune regeneration ☐

    B Beach reprofiling ☐   **D** Coastal realignment ☑ **(1 mark)**

> **Guided**

(b) Beach nourishment is an example of a soft engineering technique that helps protect coasts from erosion.

State **one** advantage and **one** disadvantage of beach nourishment.

Advantage: Beach nourishment widens beaches so they provide more

protection to the coast.

Disadvantage: Beach nourishment requires a lot

of maintenance.

(2 marks)

> **Guided**

(c) Explain how dune regeneration helps to prevent coastal erosion.

Dune regeneration usually involves creating new dunes or stabilising

older dunes that have become eroded. Dunes are effective at reducing

coastal erosion because they help build up

the beach without disrupting the

natural movements of the waves

Dunes gradually stabilise sandy beaches helping to prevent coastal

erosion because they plant vegetation, such as

Marram grass, which absorbs the wave's

energy. **(4 marks)**

2 Suggest **two** reasons why environmentalists prefer to use soft engineering rather than hard engineering.

> Environmental reasons are primarily about **impacts** on the environment, not economic costs.

Reason 1: Soft engineering reduce

the effects of flooding and erosion

without disrupting the natural

processes of the sea.

Reason 2: Soft engineering encourages the

formation of new habitats instead

of destroying them by using hard

engineering **(4 marks)**

Had a go ☐   Nearly there ☐   Nailed it! ☐

⊕Named example Coastal management

1   Study **Figure 1**, a map showing coastal management strategies for the Isle of Wight.

Figure 1

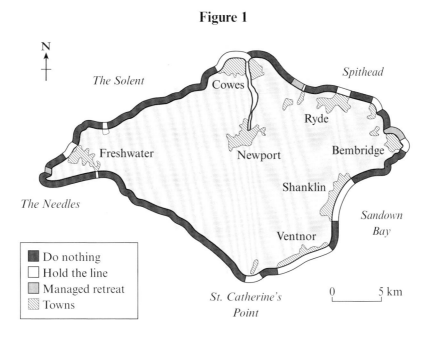

Guided

Give **one** example of a hard engineering strategy that could be used to 'hold the line' (try to prevent further erosion) in the Isle of Wight.

A sea wall – this would prevent further erosion of the coast to 'hold

the line'.   **(1 mark)**

2   Explain the costs and benefits of a 'do nothing' approach to coastal management.

> Remember that costs can mean more than just financial costs – it can mean a range of disadvantages including environmental, political and social costs.

....

....

....

....

....

....

....

....

....

....

....

....   **(6 marks)**

$\dfrac{5}{7}$

River valleys

Only revise 'River landscapes' if it is one of the options you studied.

Guided

1   The sentences below describe the way a river's long profile and cross profile change over its course. Complete the sentences using terms from the box.

> Read all the items in the box carefully first, thinking about what each one means.

~~upland~~	cross profile	long profile	steep
flat	lowland	vertical	lateral

Rivers begin in ....upland........ areas and flow downhill. Near the source, the

long profile of a river shows a steep gradient. It gradually gets lower and

less ....steep........ until the river reaches sea level. The river has a V-shaped

cross profile in the upper course. By the time the river reaches its lower

course, the valley is wide and ....flat........ .

(2 marks)

2   Study **Figure 1**, a long profile diagram which shows how the shape of a river valley changes as it moves down the slope.

Figure 1

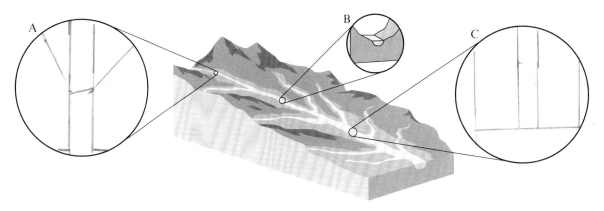

(a)   Complete **Figure 1** by sketching the shape of the valley at points **A** and **C** in the spaces provided.

~~(2 marks)~~

(b)   The contour patterns below show what the valley looks like at different points on **Figure 1**. Place the letters **A**, **B** and **C** in the boxes below each contour pattern to indicate where it would occur on the long profile.

(i) 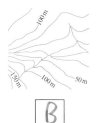   (ii)    (iii)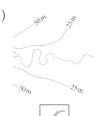

(i) B   (ii) A   (iii) C

(3 marks)

River processes

1 Study **Figure 1**, a diagram showing the different ways a river transports its load.

Figure 1

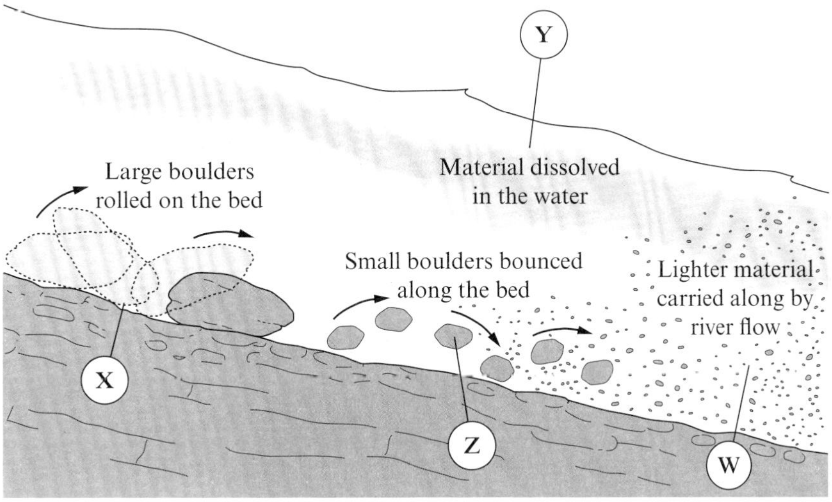

Y — Material dissolved in the water

Large boulders rolled on the bed — X

Small boulders bounced along the bed — Z

Lighter material carried along by river flow — W

(a) Name the process labelled by the letter **Z** on **Figure 1**.

> Remember that there are four river transportation processes: traction, saltation, suspension and solution.

Saltation

(1 mark)

> Guided

(b) Explain **one** reason why rivers deposit sediment.

When a river loses energy (slows down), *some sediment that it carries is deposited because they are too heavy.*

(2 marks)

> Guided

2 Compare the processes of abrasion and attrition.

Both abrasion and attrition are forms of erosion but they erode material in different ways.

Abrasion is ....

....

....

Attrition is *Sharp rocks become eroded*

....

....

....

(4 marks)

Erosion landforms

1 Study **Figure 1**, which shows the upper course of a river.

Figure 1

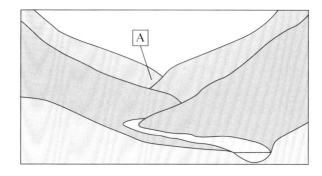

Which **one** of the following is the name of the feature **A** in **Figure 1**?

A Interlocking spur ☐

B Gorge ☐

C Meander ☐

D Levee ☐

(1 mark)

> **Guided**

2 (a) **Figure 2** shows a cross section through a waterfall. Complete the labels on this diagram.

Figure 2

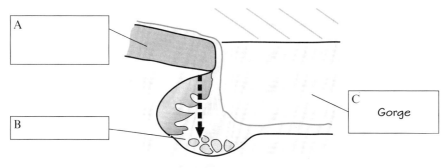

A

B

C
Gorge

(2 marks)

(b) Explain why rock type is important in the formation of a waterfall.

Make sure you refer to **hard** and **soft** rock in your answer.

....

....

....

....

....

.... (4 marks)

Erosion and deposition landforms

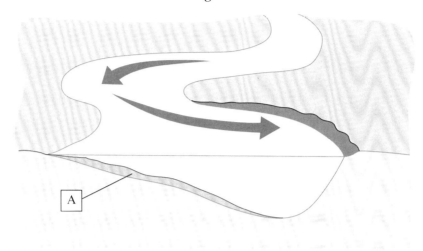

> **Guided**

1 Study **Figure 1**, which shows a cross section through a meander.

Figure 1

57

State the main process that would occur at point **A** on **Figure 1**.

Deposition   **(1 mark)**

2 Study **Figure 2**, which shows a cross section through a meander.

Figure 2

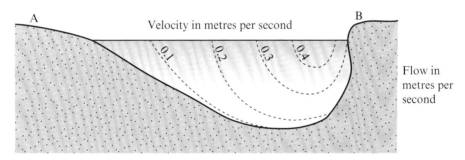

Describe the relationship between river depth and velocity on a meander.

> For this question, you should try to quote figures from the diagram to support your answer.

....

....

....   **(2 marks)**

Deposition landforms

Guided 1 Explain why deposition occurs in the lower course of the river.

> Make sure you comment on the size of the sediment (alluvium) that gets deposited first – and say why!

The gradient of the river is at its lowest in the lower course of the river.

This ....

....

....

....

....

....

(4 marks)

2 Explain the formation of a natural levee. You may draw diagrams in the box below to help.

> Remember that the formation of a levee is a gradual process, which happens as a result of repeated floods. The terms **alluvium**, **heaviest**, **transport** and **embankment** will be useful.

....

....

....

....

....

....

....

....

(4 marks)

Named example **River landforms**

1 Study **Figure 1**, a 1:50 000 map extract showing a section of the River Esk near Carlisle, Cumbria.

Figure 1

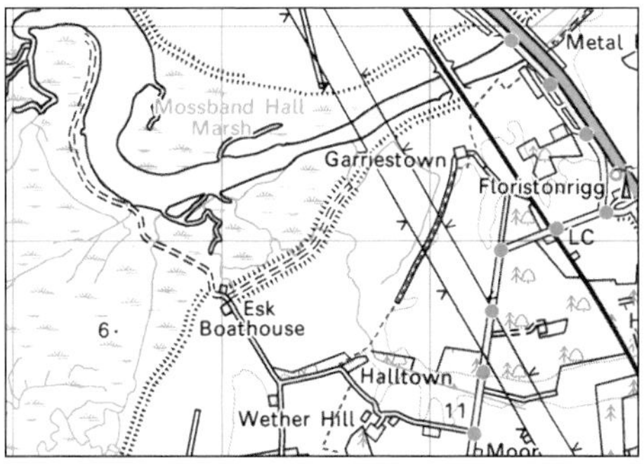

Ordnance Survey Maps, © Crown copyright 2017, OS 100030901 and supplied by courtesy of Maps International.

Guided

(a) Identify which part of the River Esk's course **Figure 1** shows, by selecting **one** of the following.

A Upper course   ☐

B Middle course ☐

C Lower course   ☑   **(1 mark)**

(b) What is the name of the river landform shown in this extract?

.... **(1 mark)**

2 (a) Give **one** example of a major erosion or deposition landform found on a river you have studied.

River name: ....

Major landform: .... **(2 marks)**

(b) Explain the formation of this landform.

....

....

....

....

.... **(4 marks)**

Flood risk factors

1 Study **Figure 1**, a diagram showing discharge after the same rainstorm in two drainage basins.

Figure 1

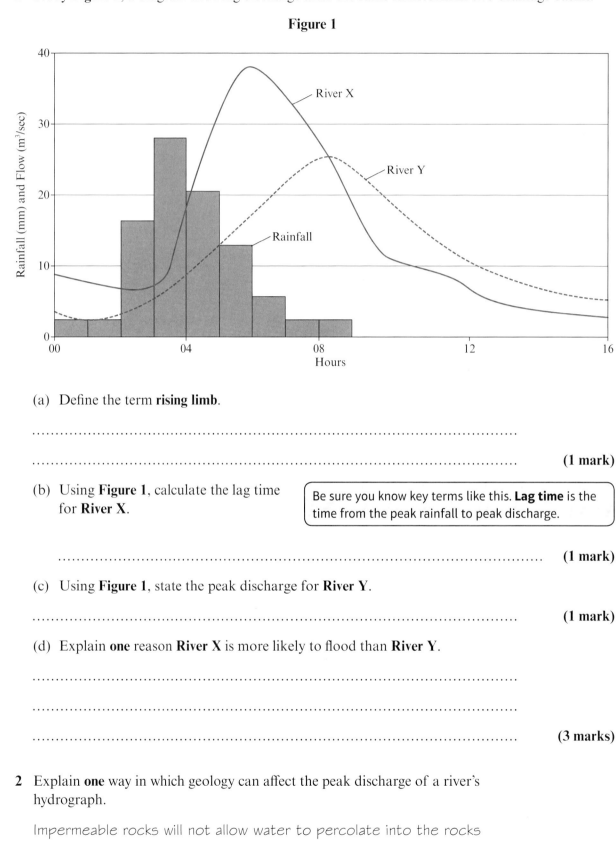

(a) Define the term **rising limb**.

....

.... **(1 mark)**

(b) Using **Figure 1**, calculate the lag time for **River X**.

| Be sure you know key terms like this. **Lag time** is the time from the peak rainfall to peak discharge. |

.... **(1 mark)**

(c) Using **Figure 1**, state the peak discharge for **River Y**.

.... **(1 mark)**

(d) Explain **one** reason **River X** is more likely to flood than **River Y**.

....

....

.... **(3 marks)**

⟩Guided⟩ 2 Explain **one** way in which geology can affect the peak discharge of a river's hydrograph.

Impermeable rocks will not allow water to percolate into the rocks

below the ground. The water then ....

.... **(2 marks)**

Hard engineering

1 Study **Figure 1**, an aerial photograph of a hard engineering river management strategy.

Figure 1

(a) Identify the type of hard engineering shown in **Figure 1**.

     A   Channel straightening   ☐

     B   River embankment   ☐

     C   Flood relief channel   ☐

     D   Dam and reservoir   ☐   **(1 mark)**

(b) Explain how the management strategy shown in **Figure 1** works to reduce the risk of river flooding.

> For this question, think about the role that storing water plays.

....

....

.... **(2 marks)**

> **Guided**

(c) Suggest **one** possible disadvantage of the construction of this type of hard engineering management strategy for the area shown in **Figure 1**.

People may have to move away from the construction area because ......

....

.... **(2 marks)**

Soft engineering

1   Study **Figure 1**, a news article about flood defences in Boscastle, Cornwall.

Figure 1

In August 2004, the River Valency flooded Boscastle, causing huge amounts of damage. Since 2004, flood walls have been built along parts of the riverbank. The river has been widened and deepened in places. The old bridge, which trapped debris and made flooding worse in 2004, has been replaced with a new, higher and wider bridge. The village car park, which saw cars washed away during the flood, has been moved onto higher ground and hedges have been planted to divide the car park into sections. When floods came to Boscastle again in 2007, the impact was much less than in 2004.

> **Guided**

(a)   Using the information in **Figure 1**, complete the following table to show whether the flood management strategies are hard engineering solutions or soft engineering solutions. Use a tick to show your answer.   **(2 marks)**

Flood management strategies	Hard engineering	Soft engineering
(i) Building flood walls	✓	
(ii) Planting hedges to divide up the car park		
(iii) Moving the car park to a higher location		

(b)   'Both hard and soft engineering strategies have advantages for responses to major river flooding events.' Use evidence to support this statement.

Evidence here means facts and information to back up your answer. Remember that you can use **Figure 1** to provide evidence, or the example of a flood management scheme that you have studied, or both.

....

....

....

....

....

....

....

....

....

....

....

....   **(6 marks)**

⊕ Named example Flood management

> **Guided**

1 Study **Figure 1**, a map showing areas of London at risk of river flooding.

Figure 1

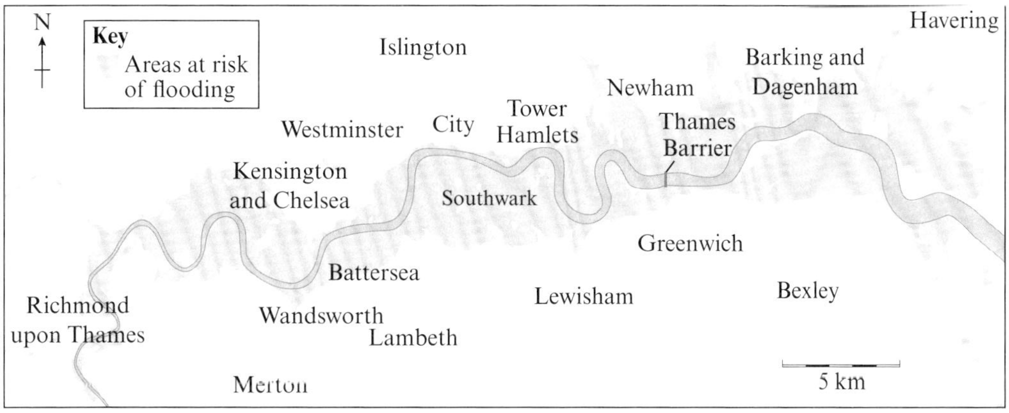

Suggest **one** social issue and **one** enviromental issue related to managing river flooding in London.

Social issue: Some areas might have hard engineering protection while others do not.

Environmental issue: ....

....

.... **(2 marks)**

2 With reference to an example of a UK flood management scheme that you have studied, explain **two** ways in which the risk of flooding has been reduced.

> Make sure that you make specific reference to a particular UK flood management scheme you have studied. This will have included the management strategy involved, which you can use to answer this question.

Name of UK flood management scheme: ....

First way: ....

....

....

....

Second way: ....

....

....

.... **(4 marks)**

Glacial processes

> Only revise 'Glacial landscapes' if it is one of the options you studied.

1   Study **Figure 1**, a photograph of a modern-day glacier in the Alps.

Figure 1

Freeze–thaw weathering

> **Guided**

(a)   Label the photograph to show where you would expect to find evidence of:

   (i)   freeze–thaw weathering

   (ii)   transportation

   (iii) deposition.   **(3 marks)**

(b)   In the box below, draw a diagram to explain how glaciers erode by **plucking**.

> It is fine to draw a series of diagrams to show stages in a process, but remember not to waste time shading in your diagram unless that is specifically asked for.

                                                                                         (2 marks)

(c)   Describe the glacial transport process known as **bulldozing**.

....

....

....   **(2 marks)**

Erosion landforms 1

> **Guided**

1 Select the correct words from this box to complete the paragraph about the formation of a corrie.

slip	expands	weathering	arete	gap	~~compacts~~	abrasion

Snow in a mountainside hollow ......compacts.... into ice. Freeze–thaw

.... around the corrie means rock falls onto the ice. These rocks help

the base of the corrie to erode. A lip forms where the ice leaves the corrie because

of rotational .... **(2 marks)**

2 Identify **two** features that would help identify a corrie on an OS map extract of a previously glaciated area.

Feature 1: ....

....

Feature 2: ....

.... **(2 marks)**

3 In the box below, draw a labelled diagram to illustrate how corries form.

> Look back at question 1 to help you with your answer.

(4 marks)

Erosion landforms 2

1   Study **Figure 1**, a photograph of a glaciated valley in the Alps mountain range.

Figure 1

(a)   Label the following two features of a glaciated valley on the photograph in **Figure 1**:

   (i)   truncated spur

   (ii) U-shaped valley.   **(2 marks)**

(b)   Draw a diagram in the box below to suggest how the valley shown in
      Figure 1 may have looked **before** glaciation.

> If you have studied river landscapes as well as glacial landscapes, you can use what you know about both
> glaciation (truncated spurs, U-shaped valleys) and river landscapes (interlocking spurs) in this answer.

                                                                                                (4 marks)

Transportation and deposition landforms

1 Study **Figure 1**, a photograph of a modern-day glacier in Switzerland.

Figure 1

Y   X

(a) Identify the landform of glacial transportation and deposition labelled **X** in **Figure 1**. Use a tick to show your answer.

> Think about the labelling. The landform type in the photograph (labelled X and Y) appear in pairs, either side of the glacier.

Landform	
Terminal moraine	
Drumlin	
Erratic	
Lateral moraine	

(1 mark)

Guided

(b) On **Figure 1**, the landform labelled **Y** is a second, higher range of ridges on either side of the glacier. Suggest how features **X** and **Y** were formed.

Landform Y probably formed when the glacier was wider than it is currently.

Like X, landform Y is ....

....

....

....

(4 marks)

67

🌐 Named example Upland glaciated area

1   Study **Figure 1**, an OS map extract of the Langdale Valley in the Lake District (1:50 000 scale enlarged).

Figure 1

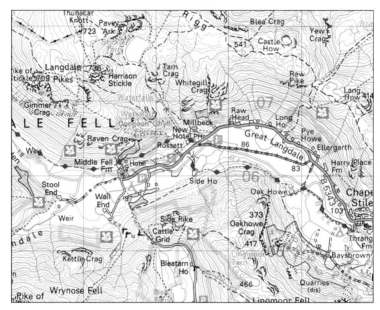

Ordnance Survey Maps. © Crown copyright 2017, OS 100030901 and supplied by courtesy of Maps International.

Describe and explain the evidence you can see in this map extract that suggests that the Langdale Valley has been glaciated.

> Make sure that you use grid references or named locations from the map.

....

....

....

....

....

....

....

....

....

....

....

....   **(6 marks)**

Activities and conflicts

<Guided> **1** Study **Figure 1**, a forested area in Snowdonia National Park, UK.

Figure 1

Describe **two** economic activities that could take
place in an upland glaciated landscape like the
one shown in **Figure 1**.

> Think about the different economic
> activities in glaciated upland areas
> that you have studied, such as tourism,
> farming, forestry and quarrying.

Economic activity 1: Forestry could take place in this upland glaciated

landscape: conifer trees could be grown for wood. ....

....

Economic activity 2: ....

....

....

.... **(4 marks)**

<Guided> **2** Suggest **one** reason why there could be a conflict over land use between forestry
and conservation in an upland glaciated area like Snowdonia.

Conservation means keeping natural habitats in upland glaciated areas

but forestry ....

....

.... **(2 marks)**

Named example Tourism

>**Guided**> 1 Study **Figure 1**, a photograph of a popular tourist destination in the Lake District, a glaciated upland area in the UK.

Figure 1

Suggest **two** ways in which tourism might put pressure on the physical environment shown in **Figure 1**.

> Think about the three main groups of impacts from tourism: social, economic and environmental. **Environmental** impacts will be the ones to focus on for this question because it asks about the **physical** environment.

Way 1: Footpath erosion from large numbers of visitors.

Way 2: ....

....

....   **(4 marks)**

2 For an example of a glaciated upland area in the UK that you have studied, explain **one** way in which the impact of tourism on the landscape can be reduced through management strategies.

Name of glaciated upland area: ....

....

....

....

....

....

....   **(3 marks)**

Global urban change

1 What is meant by the term **urbanisation**?

.... **(1 mark)**

2 Study **Figure 1**, a graph showing urbanisation trends in major regions of the world, 1950–2050.

Figure 1

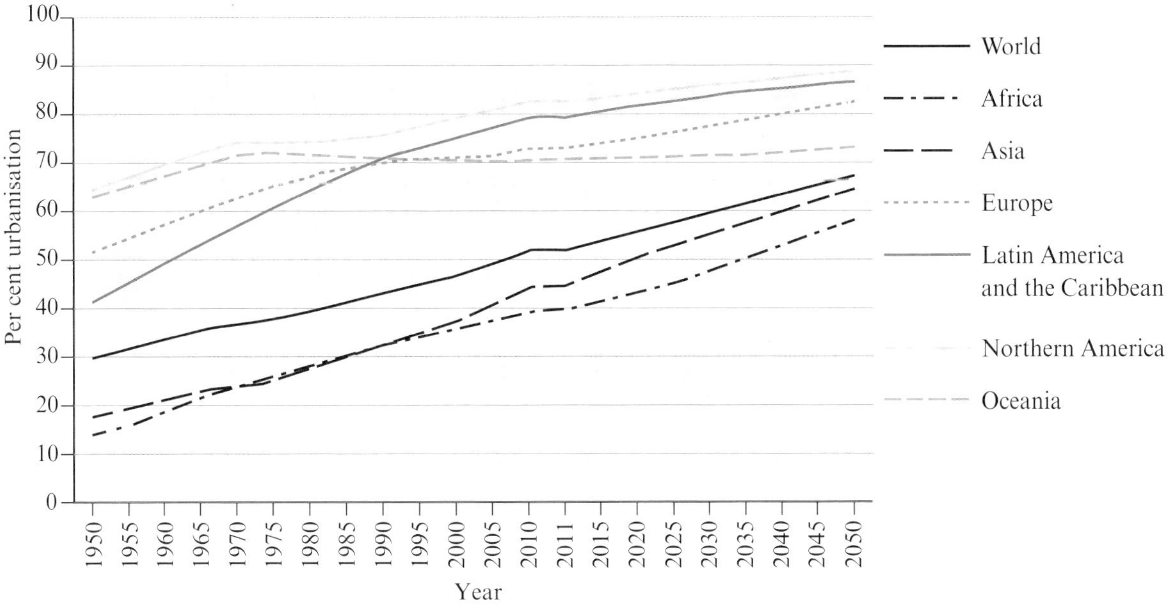

(a) According to **Figure 1**, in the year 2000, what percentage of the world's population lived in urban areas?

.... **(1 mark)**

(b) According to **Figure 1**, what is the likely projected urban population increase for Africa between 1950 and 2050?

    A 12 per cent   ☐

    B 46 per cent   ☐

    C 53 per cent   ☐

    D 88 per cent   ☐ **(1 mark)**

⟩ Guided ⟩

(c) Using the information in **Figure 1**, compare the projected urbanisation trends of the HIC regions with NEE and LIC regions.

> When **comparing**, use linking words and phrases such as 'while', 'whereas', 'on the other hand' or 'in contrast'.

In North America and Europe (HICs) the rate of

urbanisation is projected to be slower, whereas ....

....

.... **(2 marks)**

Urbanisation factors

1 Which **one** of the following statements best describes a megacity?

  A A city with a population of more than 5 million ☐

  B A city with a population of 8–10 million ☐

  C A city with a population of more than 10 million ☐

  D A city with a population of more than 20 million ☐ **(1 mark)**

> **Guided** >   2 Study **Figure 1**, which shows the distribution of megacities in 2015.

Figure 1

Describe the distribution of megacities shown in **Figure 1**.

> Try to refer to specific parts of the world and any patterns you can see.

Most of the megacities shown are in Asia, 12 of the 21. Most are

found in ....

....

....

.... **(3 marks)**

> **Guided** >   3 State **two** factors that help explain rapid urbanisation in LICs and NEEs.

Factor 1: High rates of rural–urban migration.

Factor 2: ....

.... **(2 marks)**

🌐 Case study **Non-UK city: location and growth**

1 (a) You have studied a major city in an LIC or NEE as a case study. Describe your city's location.

> Try to include: where in the country the major city is, using compass directions; whether it is on the coast, or a major river; its connections to other cities.

Name of city: ....

....

....

....

....   **(2 marks)**

(b) Explain **one** reason why the location of the major city you have studied has been important for its growth.

> Does it have a coastal location that has enabled a port to develop and trade? Does it have certain resources that mean particular industries have grown and attracted workers?

....

....

....

....   **(2 marks)**

⟩ Guided ⟩

2 One factor influencing rapid urbanisation in cities in LICs and NEEs is a high rate of natural increase. Give **two** reasons for this.

Reason 1: High natural increase occurs when birth rates are high and

death rates are falling. One reason for this is ....

....

....

....

Reason 2: ....

....

....

....   **(4 marks)**

🌐 Case study   **Non-UK city: opportunities**

1   Study **Figure 1**, a photograph showing women selling street food in Mexico City, a major city in an NEE.

Figure 1

(a)   Explain what is meant by **the informal employment sector** in growing cities in LICs and NEEs.

> You can use brief, relevant examples, even if the question does not ask for them. For example, here you might refer to informal sector jobs such as selling street food, car washing, hairdressing or recycling.

....

....

....

....   **(2 marks)**

Guided

(b)   Explain **two** ways in which urban growth has created opportunities for people who have recently migrated to a growing city in an LIC or NEE.

> **Social** opportunities include access to services and access to resources. **Economic** opportunities include the jobs generated by growing industrial areas and growing service areas.

First way: Urban growth has given people greater access to the sorts of services shared by communities, such as clean water supplies and proper sanitation.

Second way: ....

....

....   **(4 marks)**

🌐 Case study **Non-UK city: challenges 1**

1   Study **Figure 1**, a sketch of housing in a squatter settlement in Dhaka.

Figure 1

A student has written labels for the five letters, **A–E**. The labels are listed below. Which **two** of these labels represent challenges of managing environmental issues in slums and squatter settlements?

> Read the question carefully. Here you are being asked to look only for the **environmental** issues involved.

A   Some squatter settlements have access to electricity.   ☐

B   Houses are made of several different types of materials.   ☐

C   Rubbish is left by the roadside, which attracts rats.   ☐

D   The housing is often too small for the numbers of people
        living there, leading to overcrowding.   ☐

E   Residents have to rely on open water sources for water and
        for sanitation, so they become very polluted.   ☐   **(2 marks)**

⟩ **Guided** ⟩   2   Discuss the challenges of slums or squatter settlements for an LIC or NEE city
                    that you have studied.

Name of city: ....

Rapid urban growth in LICs and NEEs means that many

people coming to the city cannot find suitable housing,

which leads to overcrowding in old, unsafe housing (slums)

> Continue your answer on your own paper. You should aim to write about half a side of A4.

or people making shacks to live in on unoccupied bits of land in and

around the city (squatter settlements). ....

....

....

....

....

....   **(6 marks)**

> Continue your answer on your own paper. You should aim to write about half a side of A4.

🌐 Case study **Non-UK city: challenges 2**

1   Study **Figure 1**, a text extract about congestion in Mexico City.

Figure 1

Car congestion in Mexico City

The population of Mexico City is increasing rapidly, and car ownership is also increasing – at 4.2 per cent per year. Traffic congestion is causing more and more serious economic, social and environmental challenges in the city. Almost 1000 people were killed in traffic accidents in Mexico City alone in 2012. Vehicles are responsible for 49 per cent of the greenhouse gases produced by the city.

Approximately 850 000 trips are made in the Santa Fe business district of Mexico City every day. 64 per cent of these are work-related trips. 46 per cent of commuters travel by bus, but the buses are crowded, dirty and unsafe so anyone who can afford to, travels by car. The costs in time and money are high. Commuters spend an average of 26 days a year travelling to and from the Santa Fe district. This is more days than they spend on annual holidays. Car drivers spend approximately US$1700 on fuel and car maintenance a year commuting to Santa Fe district – twice as much as bus commuters spend.

This increase in private car travel is also a challenge for businesses, who are having to increase their car parking areas. On average, companies allocate 42 per cent of their land to parking areas. This land could have been used instead to expand operations, creating more jobs.

〉 **Guided** 〉

(a)   Describe **two** problems caused by car congestion in Mexico City, as outlined in **Figure 1**.

First problem: Almost half of the greenhouse gases emitted in Mexico City come from vehicles. This is linked to car congestion because emissions are increased when cars are stuck in slow-moving traffic jams.

Second problem: ....

.... **(2 marks)**

(b)   Using your own knowledge about managing the impacts of traffic congestion in LIC or NEE cities, suggest **two** ways in which the car congestion problems described in **Figure 1** could be managed.

> If bus services in this part of Mexico City are not providing what commuters need, how could they be improved?

First way: ....

....

....

....

Second way: ....

....

....

.... **(4 marks)**

🌐 Named example **Planning for the urban poor**

1　Study **Figure 1** and **Figure 2**, artist's impressions of unplanned and planned
urban neighbourhoods in Kenya, Africa.

Figure 1

Figure 2

Guided

(a)　Suggest **two** reasons why the unplanned
neighbourhood shown in **Figure 1** would
benefit from regeneration.

> Use the information in both pictures to help
> you. What has been improved in the planned
> neighbourhood? What problems can you
> identify in the unplanned neighbourhood?

First reason: The buildings in the unplanned neighbourhood look like they
are made with flimsy materials like corrugated iron. Regeneration would
replace or repair these buildings so they were not in danger of falling down.

Second reason: ....

....

.... **(4 marks)**

(b)　The picture of the planned neighbourhood in **Figure 2** shows the results of a
participatory urban planning scheme, in which local residents were involved
in making the changes they wanted for their neighbourhood.

Explain **two** advantages of involving local
people in urban planning that is designed to
improve quality of life for the urban poor.

> Try thinking about the disadvantages of top-
> down management schemes for this question.

First advantage: ....

....

....

....

Second advantage: ....

....

....

.... **(4 marks)**

Had a go ☐ Nearly there ☐ Nailed it! ☐

Urban UK

Guided

1 Study **Figure 1**, which shows a map of the UK's population density.

Figure 1

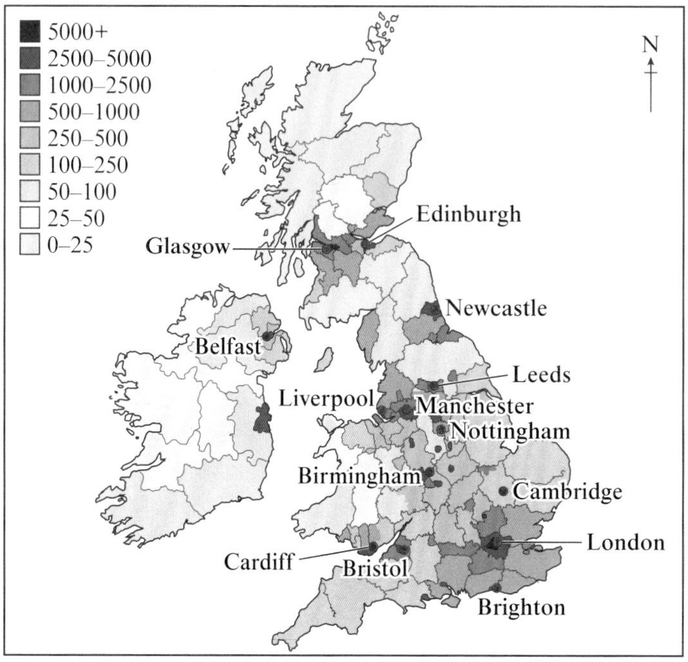

i) Northern Scotland has a relatively low population density because ....

....

....

....

ii) London has a relatively high population density because ....

....

....

....

Compare the population density of Northern Scotland and London by completing the **two boxes** on **Figure 1**. **(2 marks)**

2 Identify which **two** of the following are major urban centres in the UK.

A Birmingham ☐

B Stroud ☐

C Leeds ☐

D Malham ☐ **(2 marks)**

3 Explain **two** factors that influence the distribution of population in the UK.

> Remember that population **distribution** and population **density** are different – though the two are related. Locations with high population densities are not usually found in areas of low population, as the high densities would increase the population size. Think about physical and economic factors for your answer.

First factor: ....

....

....

Second factor: ....

....

.... **(4 marks)**

🌐 **Case study** **UK city: location and migration**

1   Study **Figure 1**, a graph of population change in the West Midlands, 2008–2009.

Figure 1

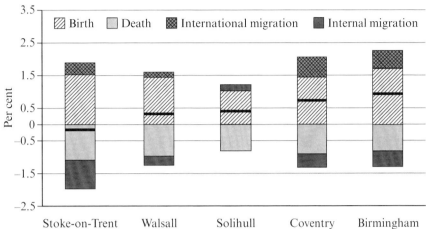

(a) In **Figure 1**, which **one** of the following regions experienced the largest population increase in 2008–2009?

   A   Birmingham   ☐   C   Walsall   ☐

   B   Stoke-on-Trent   ☐   D   Solihull   ☐   **(1 mark)**

(b) Using **Figure 1**, calculate the net population change (per cent) for Birmingham during 2008–2009.

   ....   **(1 mark)**

> **Guided**

2   Using **Figure 1** and a case study of a major city in the UK that you have studied, discuss the impacts of international migration on city growth.

> You can use **Figure 1** to identify the contribution of international migration to cities in the West Midlands, then use your knowledge to explore the impacts that international migration has had in your case study city.

Name of case study city: ....

International migration has had the most impact in Birmingham and

Coventry out of the five West Midlands cities in Figure 1. In Coventry,

for example, it has contributed 0.5 per cent to the 2 per cent growth

between 2008 and 2009. Figure 1 only shows growth over one year.

In the case of my case study city, ...

....

....

....

....   **(6 marks)**

Continue your answer on your own paper. You should aim to write about half a side of A4.

🌐 Case study UK city: opportunities

1 Study **Figure 1**, which shows a plan for urban greening a city block.

Figure 1

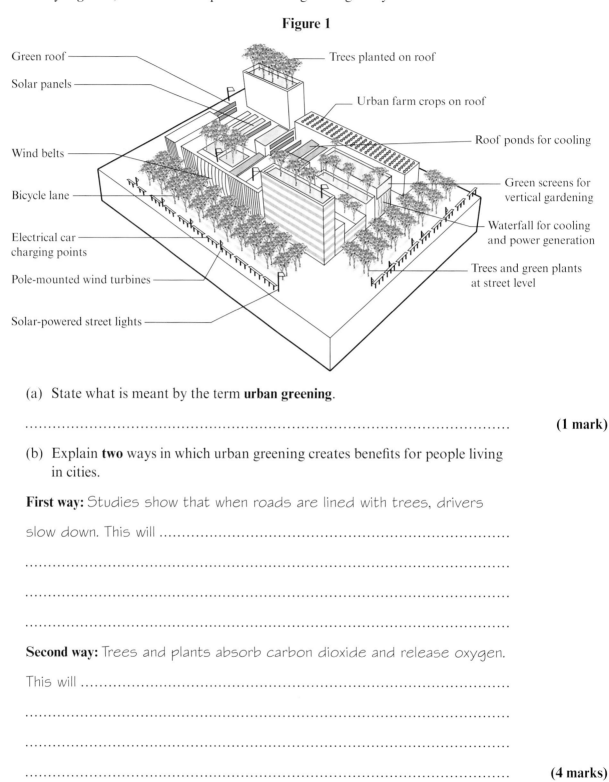

Green roof ——————— Trees planted on roof

Solar panels ——————— Urban farm crops on roof

Wind belts ——————— Roof ponds for cooling

Bicycle lane ——————— Green screens for vertical gardening

Electrical car charging points ——————— Waterfall for cooling and power generation

Pole-mounted wind turbines ——————— Trees and green plants at street level

Solar-powered street lights

(a) State what is meant by the term **urban greening**.

.... **(1 mark)**

> **Guided**

(b) Explain **two** ways in which urban greening creates benefits for people living in cities.

First way: Studies show that when roads are lined with trees, drivers

slow down. This will ....

....

....

....

Second way: Trees and plants absorb carbon dioxide and release oxygen.

This will ....

....

....

.... **(4 marks)**

2 Suggest **one** way in which urban greening could create opportunities for people living in a UK city that you have studied.

> Think about opportunities for people to improve their lives (physically or mentally) or gain new skills.

....

.... **(2 marks)**

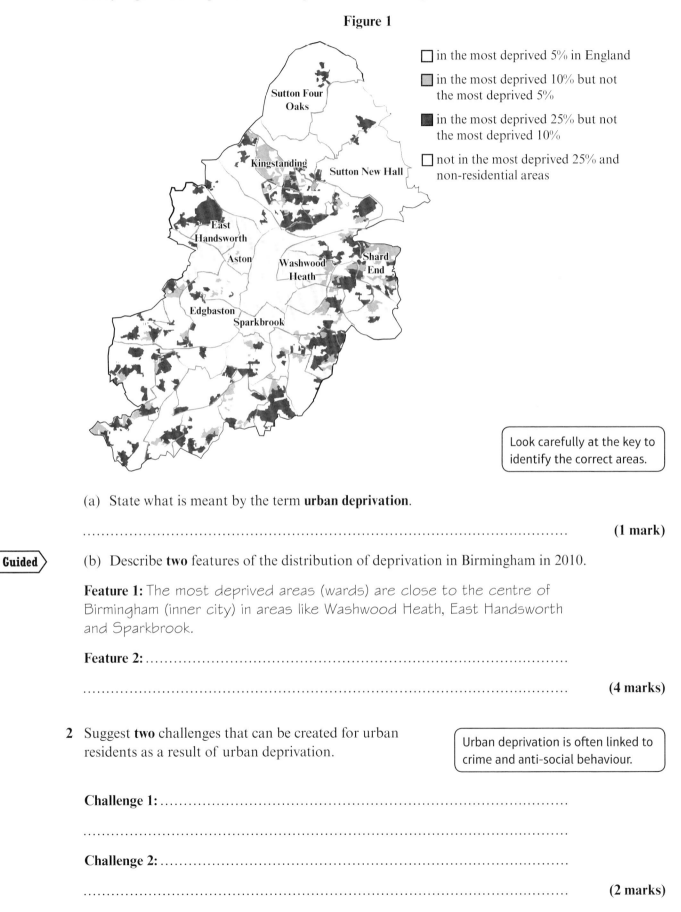 UK city: challenges 1

1   Study **Figure 1**, a map of areas of deprivation in Birmingham in 2010.

Figure 1

☐ in the most deprived 5% in England

▨ in the most deprived 10% but not the most deprived 5%

■ in the most deprived 25% but not the most deprived 10%

☐ not in the most deprived 25% and non-residential areas

Sutton Four Oaks

Kingstanding

Sutton New Hall

East Handsworth

Aston

Washwood Heath

Shard End

Edgbaston

Sparkbrook

> Look carefully at the key to identify the correct areas.

(a)   State what is meant by the term **urban deprivation**.

.... **(1 mark)**

Guided

(b)   Describe **two** features of the distribution of deprivation in Birmingham in 2010.

Feature 1: The most deprived areas (wards) are close to the centre of Birmingham (inner city) in areas like Washwood Heath, East Handsworth and Sparkbrook.

Feature 2: ....

.... **(4 marks)**

2   Suggest **two** challenges that can be created for urban residents as a result of urban deprivation.

> Urban deprivation is often linked to crime and anti-social behaviour.

Challenge 1: ....

....

Challenge 2: ....

.... **(2 marks)**

🌐 Case study **UK city: challenges 2**

1 Study **Figure 1**, a 1: 50 000 OS map extract of the Oxfordshire town of Bicester.

Figure 1

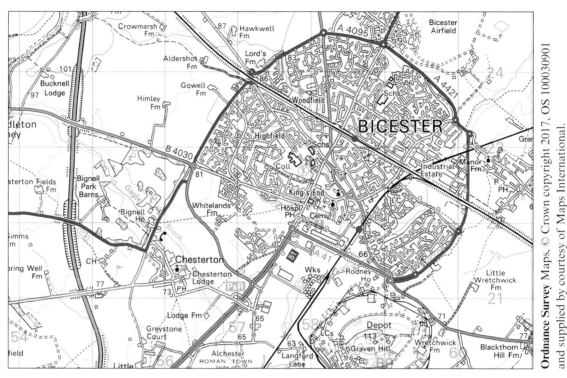

Ordnance Survey Maps, © Crown copyright 2017, OS 100030901 and supplied by courtesy of Maps International.

(a) Bicester has two rail stations, Bicester North and Bicester Village. Using **Figure 1**, which **two** of the following map references are correct for the two stations?

> To help you answer this question, think about the right way to express grid references. Which numbers do you give first: those on the horizontal easting line or those on the vertical northing line?

    A 587219 ☐   **D** 231587 ☐

    B 587231 ☐   **E** 572240 ☐   **(2 marks)**

    C 219587 ☐

> **Guided**

(b) Bicester is a popular place to live for people working in London, Birmingham or Oxford. Suggest **two** reasons why a town like Bicester becomes a commuter settlement.

First reason: Property prices in cities like London and Oxford can make it too expensive for people to buy or rent housing where they work. Cheaper property prices in a nearby town could be a reason for the development of a commuter settlement.

Second reason: ....

....

.... **(4 marks)**

(c) Suggest **one** likely impact for Bicester of it becoming a popular commuter settlement.

....

.... **(2 marks)**

🌐 Named example **UK urban regeneration**

1   Evaluate the effectiveness of an urban regeneration project you have studied.

> Some 9-mark questions will also be assessed for spelling, punctuation and grammar: SPaG. The best answers are correctly spelled and punctuated all the way through, use good grammar so the answer is easy to understand, and use a wide range of specialist vocabulary. Think about the distinctive specialist terms associated with urban regeneration, such as reclamation, brownfield, urban greening, urban decline, deprivation, gentrification, rebranding, social housing, private investment and sustainable transport.

....

....

....

....

....

....

....

....

....

....

....

....

....

....

....

....

....

....

....

....

....

....

(9 marks + 3 marks for SPaG)

> Continue your answer on your own paper. You should aim to write about one side of A4.

Sustainable urban living

1 Study **Figure 1**, which shows a smart meter for monitoring household energy use.

Figure 1

> **Guided**

(a) Explain **one** way in which a household energy meter could help with energy conservation in UK cities.

An energy meter means people can see how much the energy they are

using is costing. This would encourage people to use less energy because

....

....

....   **(2 marks)**

(b) Explain **two** further ways in which energy conservation can be increased in urban areas.

> Remember that energy conservation is about using less energy. Think about what happens in urban areas: in offices, in the streets, in homes. You might also think about incentives that could be used.

First way: ....

....

Second way: ....

....

....   **(4 marks)**

2 Identify **one** way in which water conservation can be increased in urban areas.

....

....

....

....   **(2 marks)**

Urban transport strategies

1 Study **Figure 1**, which provides information about London's congestion charge scheme.

Figure 1

> London's congestion charge was introduced in February 2003 with the aim of reducing traffic congestion in London – the worst of all UK cities for traffic congestion.
>
> **How does it work?**
>
> The congestion charge is an £11.50 (in 2017) payment that allows motorists to drive into and out of the central zone of London as many times as they want within one day. Cameras around the charging zone record the number plates of all vehicles in the zone and match them against a database. People who haven't paid are charged £14 the next day, which rises to £130 if unpaid that day. People who live in the charging zone don't have to pay the congestion charge, nor do taxi drivers, buses, motorcyclists or cyclists.
>
> **How successful has it been?**
>
> • All money raised by the congestion charge has to be spent on improving London's transport.
> • Each day, around 80 000 fewer cars enter the charging zone than they did per day in 2002.
> • The numbers of people cycling in London has increased by 66 per cent since 2003.
> • However, traffic speeds during London's busiest times are actually slower than in 2002. This may be because roads have been narrowed in order to fit in bus lanes and cycle lanes.

(a) Identify which **two** of these statements about London's congestion charge are confirmed by the information in **Figure 1**.

   A There have been significant reductions in CO_2 emissions as a result of the congestion charge.   ☐

   B Because the number of cars has been reduced, congestion has been reduced.   ☐

   C Peak time traffic congestion, as measured by vehicle speeds, is actually now worse than before the congestion charge was introduced.   ☐

   D Taxi drivers have been the biggest opponents of the congestion charge scheme because it has cost taxi companies more than £1.2 billion in fines since the congestion charge was introduced.   ☐

   E Cycling in London has increased by 66 per cent since the introduction of the congestion charge.   ☐   **(2 marks)**

Guided

(b) Suggest **two** ways in which the introduction of the congestion charge contributed to the numbers of people cycling in London.

> Think about what the money from the congestion charge scheme is used for in London: there is information about this in **Figure 1**.

First way: People who drove short distances from their homes outside the congestion charge zone to work in central London would save a lot of money by cycling as bikes do not have to pay the congestion charge.

Second way: ....

....

....   **(2 marks)**

Measuring development 1

1 Study **Figure 1**, a scattergraph comparing infant mortality with GDP per head (similar to GNI per head).

Figure 1

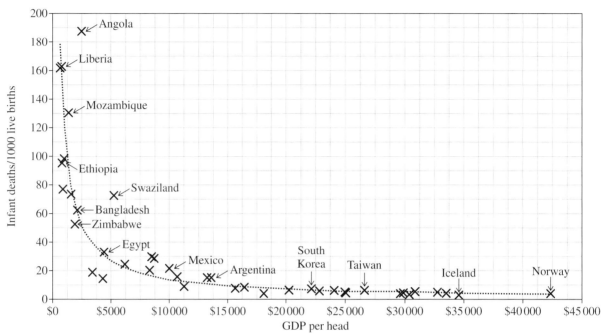

(a) Which **one** of the following countries is an outlier from the line of best fit on the scattergraph in **Figure 1**?

> Make sure you understand specialist terms to do with different sorts of graphs. Here, **outlier** means a point that lies away from the main group or trend.

A   Liberia   ☐

B   Ethiopia   ☐

C   Swaziland   ☐

D   Taiwan   ☐

(1 mark)

⟩ **Guided** ⟩ (b) Identify the relationship between income (GDP per head) and infant mortality shown in the scattergraph?

> By **relationship** this question means any link between the two factors.

The relationship is a negative (inverse) one, so ....

.... **(1 mark)**

(c) Identify **two** limitations of using a single development measure to indicate how developed a country is.

Limitation 1: ....

....

Limitation 2: ....

.... **(2 marks)**

Measuring development 2

1   Study **Figure 1**, a map classifying countries of the world according to their
    Human Development Index (HDI) score.

Figure 1

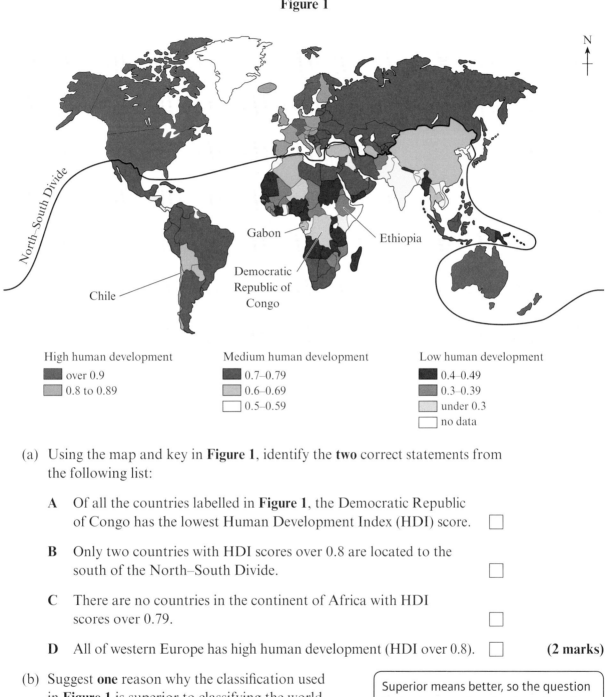

High human development
- ▣ over 0.9
- ▣ 0.8 to 0.89

Medium human development
- ▣ 0.7–0.79
- ▣ 0.6–0.69
- ☐ 0.5–0.59

Low human development
- ▣ 0.4–0.49
- ▣ 0.3–0.39
- ☐ under 0.3
- ☐ no data

(a) Using the map and key in **Figure 1**, identify the **two** correct statements from
     the following list:

A   Of all the countries labelled in **Figure 1**, the Democratic Republic
    of Congo has the lowest Human Development Index (HDI) score.   ☐

B   Only two countries with HDI scores over 0.8 are located to the
    south of the North–South Divide.   ☐

C   There are no countries in the continent of Africa with HDI
    scores over 0.79.   ☐

D   All of western Europe has high human development (HDI over 0.8).   ☐   **(2 marks)**

⟩ **Guided** ⟩

(b) Suggest **one** reason why the classification used
     in **Figure 1** is superior to classifying the world
     into rich North and poor South.

> Superior means better, so the question
> is about comparing the strengths of
> different measures of development.

Figure 1 shows that, although there are rich countries in the global

North, not all the countries in the north are rich. And in the global South

....

....

....   **(2 marks)**

The Demographic Transition Model

1 Study **Figure 1**, a diagram giving a simplified version of the Demographic Transition Model (DTM).

Figure 1

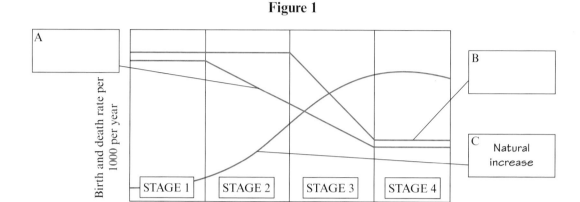

(a) Using the boxes on **Figure 1**, label:
   (i) the birth rate line
   (ii) the death rate line.

> Take care with questions like this. Think it through clearly and don't rush.

(2 marks)

> Guided

(b) Give **two** reasons for the high birth rate shown in stages 1 and 2 of the Demographic Transition Model.

Reason 1: In stage 1, the birth rate is high because lack of effective medicine and sanitation means infant death rates are very high and people have lots of children because not many survive.

Reason 2: ....
....
.... **(4 marks)**

(c) Suggest **two** reasons why birth rate drops in stage 3 of the Demographic Transition Model.

> Remember, the Demographic Transition Model describes a theory of how development has an impact on a country's population by affecting birth rates and death rates – and total population – over time.

Reason 1: ....
....

Reason 2: ....
.... **(2 marks)**

Uneven development: causes

1   Study **Figure 1**, a charity advert about the importance of access to safe water.

Figure 1

This is Kwame. He is eight years old and lives in Ghana. In the dry season, it takes two hours to walk from his home to the waterhole to get water. That means **Kwame has no time to go to school**. And the water from the waterhole is not clean. When Kwame drinks the water, **he often gets diarrhoea** and stomach pains and he is too ill to play with his friends. Sometimes, children in his village die from disease in the water.

In Ghana, 4000 children die every year from diarrhoea, all because their families don't have access to safe water.

(a) Lack of access to water is a cause of uneven development. Causes of uneven development can be classified as physical, historical and economic. State whether lack of access to water is physical, historical or economic.

.... **(1 mark)**

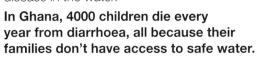

(b) Using **Figure 1** and your own knowledge, describe and explain how problems with access to water can affect people's standards of living.

> Remember that access to water involves having enough water (quantity) and having water that is safe to drink (quality).

The charity advert says that it takes two hours for Kwame to get water

from the waterhole. This means he has no time to ....

....

....

....

....

....

When Kwame is sick from drinking unsafe water, ...

....

....

....

.... **(6 marks)**

Uneven development: consequences

1   Study **Figure 1**, a newspaper article about international migration and its consequences for Peterborough, a city in the east of the UK.

Figure 1

> **Immigration to Peterborough**
>
> Schools in Peterborough are struggling with the task of teaching so many students who do not speak English as their first language. In Peterborough's primary schools, around 30 per cent of students do not speak English as their first language, 22 per cent in secondary schools – while the national average is 12 per cent. Currently around 2000 new migrants come to Peterborough each year and that can mean up to 900 new students starting in Peterborough's schools at various points in time throughout each school year – the equivalent of three new primary schools.

Guided

(a)   Give **one** reason why international migrants have decided to come to live and work in Peterborough.

People from poorer countries can earn more working in richer countries, so

....

.... **(2 marks)**

(b)   Using **Figure 1** and your own knowledge, suggest **two** impacts of large numbers of international migrants moving to Peterborough.

First impact: ....

....

....

Second impact: ....

....

.... **(4 marks)**

(c)   Suggest **one** reason why international migration is a consequence of uneven development.

> Remember that uneven development means that some countries are much poorer than others.

....

....

....

....

.... **(2 marks)**

Investment, industry and aid

1   Study **Figure 1**, a map showing the global distribution of international aid.

Figure 1

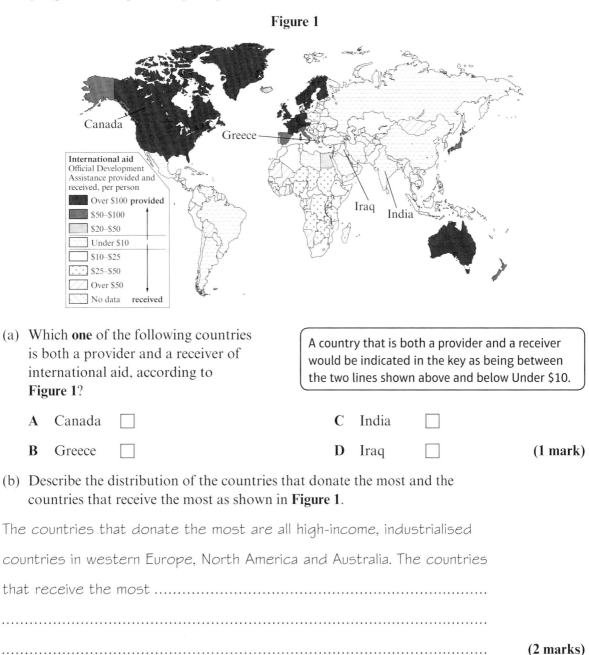

(a)   Which **one** of the following countries is both a provider and a receiver of international aid, according to **Figure 1**?

> A country that is both a provider and a receiver would be indicated in the key as being between the two lines shown above and below Under $10.

   A   Canada   ☐   **C**   India   ☐

   B   Greece   ☐   **D**   Iraq   ☐   **(1 mark)**

⟩Guided⟩   (b)   Describe the distribution of the countries that donate the most and the countries that receive the most as shown in **Figure 1**.

The countries that donate the most are all high-income, industrialised

countries in western Europe, North America and Australia. The countries

that receive the most ....

....

....   **(2 marks)**

2   Explain **one** advantage and **one** disadvantage of international aid as a strategy for closing the development gap.

> Think about the benefits of large-scale improvements and the problems some countries have making them.

   Advantage: ....

....

....

   Disadvantage: ....

....

....   **(4 marks)**

Technology, trade, relief and loans

1 Study **Figure 1**, a graph of Fair Trade banana sales in the UK.

Figure 1

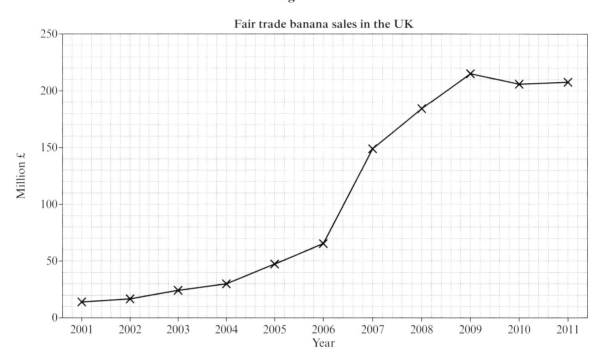

Fair trade banana sales in the UK

> **Guided**

(a) Using **Figure 1**, calculate by how much sales of Fair Trade bananas in the UK have increased between 2001 and 2011.

£208 million (2011) − .... (2001) = ...   **(1 mark)**

(b) Using **Figure 1** and your answer from (a), describe the changes in sales of Fair Trade bananas in the UK between 2001 and 2011.

....

....

....

....   **(2 marks)**

(c) Explain how Fair Trade schemes try to reduce the development gap faced by poorer countries that trade with richer countries.

> Your answer needs to identify development gap problems caused by global trade, then also how Fair Trade schemes try to reduce the gap for LICs.

....

....

....

....

....

....   **(4 marks)**

🌐 Named example **Tourism**

1 Study **Figure 1**, a text extract describing part of the Kenyan National Tourism Policy.

Figure 1

> Kenya's tourism industry has always been based on beach holidays and wildlife safaris. But Kenya can also offer a wide range of other types of holiday, such as golf, mountaineering, rock climbing, birdwatching, whitewater rafting, horse riding and camel treks. Kenya also has an extremely rich and interesting culture that many tourists would find fascinating.
>
> At the moment, most tourists visit a small number of places in Kenya: the beach resorts and the game parks. Developing cultural tourism would mean we could spread tourism to new areas, away from the most visited and sometimes overcrowded areas. Developing cultural tourism would also help local people more because tourists like to buy handicraft products, such as wood carvings, beadwork and paintings.

(a) According to **Figure 1**, what sort of holidays do most tourists go to Kenya for at the moment?

.... **(1 mark)**

> Guided

(b) Suggest **two** reasons why the Kenyan government might want to expand the places that tourists visit in Kenya.

> Tourism in Kenya doesn't just help the national economy, it also helps the local economy where tourists visit. For this question, think about why encouraging tourists to go to new areas, for different sorts of holidays, would be something the government might want to encourage.

Reason 1: More places for tourists to visit would mean more tourists visiting Kenya. When tourists come from countries like China, Russia, the UK and the USA, they pay for their trips in foreign currency, which is worth a lot in Kenya. This money is very important to the national economy.

Reason 2:..

....

....

.... **(4 marks)**

2 Using an example you have studied, describe and explain how the growth of tourism has helped to reduce the development gap in an LIC or NEE.

....

....

....

....

....

.... **(6 marks)**

> Continue your answer on your own paper. You should aim to write about half a side of A4.

🌐 Case study LIC or NEE country: location and context

1 Describe the location of the LIC or NEE country that you studied in your case study.

> Try to include the continent, neighbouring countries, main physical and human features (such as mountains, rivers, coasts and cities), and transport links.

Name of country: ....

....

....

....

.... **(2 marks)**

2 Describe **one** important feature of the cultural context of the LIC or NEE that you have studied.

> For this answer, pick one cultural aspect of the country you have studied and describe how it is important: for example, Bollywood is an important part of India's culture and means that many millions of people around the world are influenced by Indian films.

....

....

....

.... **(2 marks)**

3 Describe how the industrial structure of the LIC or NEE you have studied has changed as the country has developed.

> A common feature of LIC and NEE development has been a reduction in the numbers of people working in farming and an increase in the numbers working in industry (often manufacturing) and services. Remember that the best answers include relevant detail from the case study.

....

....

....

....

....

....

....

.... **(4 marks)**

🌐 Case study LIC or NEE country: TNCs

1 Assess the advantages and disadvantages of TNCs (transnational corporations)
to one LIC or NEE host country that you have studied.

> Make sure you read the question carefully. Here, you are told to use a case study in your answer, so
> make sure you include relevant, specific and accurate facts and figures from yours (such as names and
> functions of some of the TNCs involved, numbers employed in a TNC factory), etc. Remember to add a
> conclusion weighing up the advantages and disadvantages – which is most important and why.

Name of country: ....

....

....

....

....

....

....

....

....

....

....

....

....

....

....

....

....

....

....

....

....

.... **(9 marks)**

> Continue your answer on your own paper. You should aim to write about one side of A4.

Case study LIC or NEE country: trade, politics and aid

1   Study **Figure 1**, a flow map showing volumes of global trade.

Figure 1

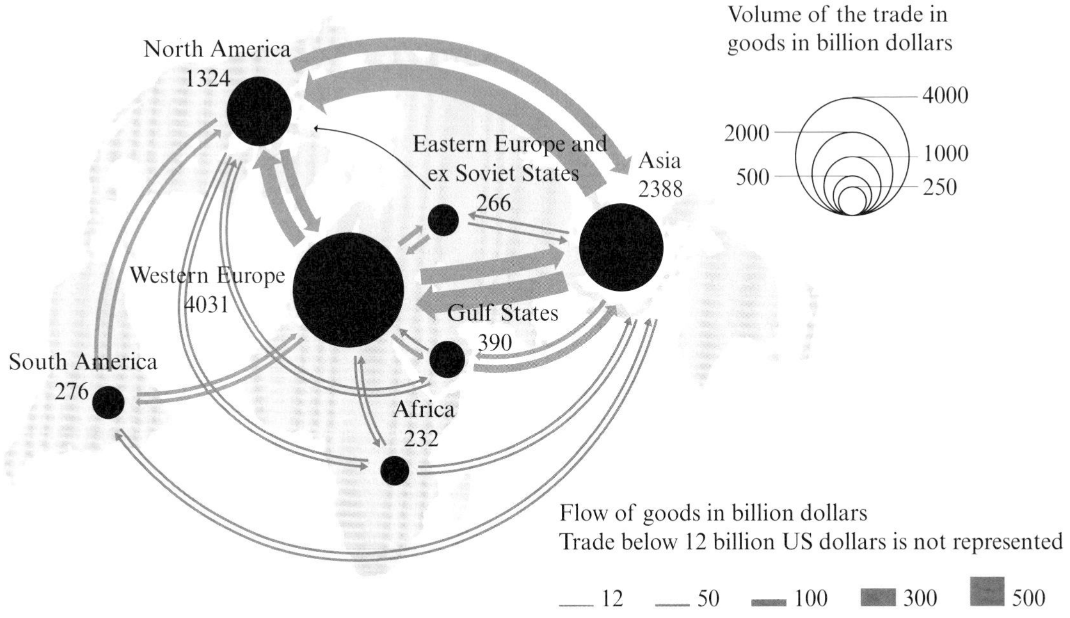

(a)   Which **one** of the following is the largest trading area shown in **Figure 1**?

A   North America   ☐

B   Asia   ☐

C   Western Europe   ☐

D   South America   ☐   **(1 mark)**

(b)   According to **Figure 1**, what is the value of Asia's exports to North America?

....   **(1 mark)**

2   Describe **one** way in which global trade has contributed to the economic development of an LIC or NEE that you have studied.

> Remember to include the name of your case study country.

Name of country: ....

....

....

....

....

....   **(3 marks)**

🌐 Case study LIC or NEE country: environmental impact

> **Guided**

1 'Economic development only has positive effects on quality of life for people in LICs and NEEs.'

Do you agree with this statement?

Yes ☐   No ☐

Justify your decision.

> This question does not specifically ask for you to use your LIC or NEE country case study knowledge, but it would be a good opportunity to, so that you can illustrate your answer with relevant examples. Remember to keep your answer focused on the relationship between quality of life and economic development. Try to consider at least two points **for** the statement and two points **against** it.

Good quality of life means a good standard of living and an increased

opportunity for people to live comfortable and healthy lives. Economic

development is the main reason for increased quality of life.

....

....

....

....

....

....

....

....

....

....

....

....

....

....

....

....   **(9 marks)**

> Continue your answer on your own paper. You should aim to write about one side of A4.

UK: deindustrialisation, globalisation and policy

1 Study **Figure 1**, a graph showing changes in output and employment in the UK coal industry, 1962–2010.

Figure 1

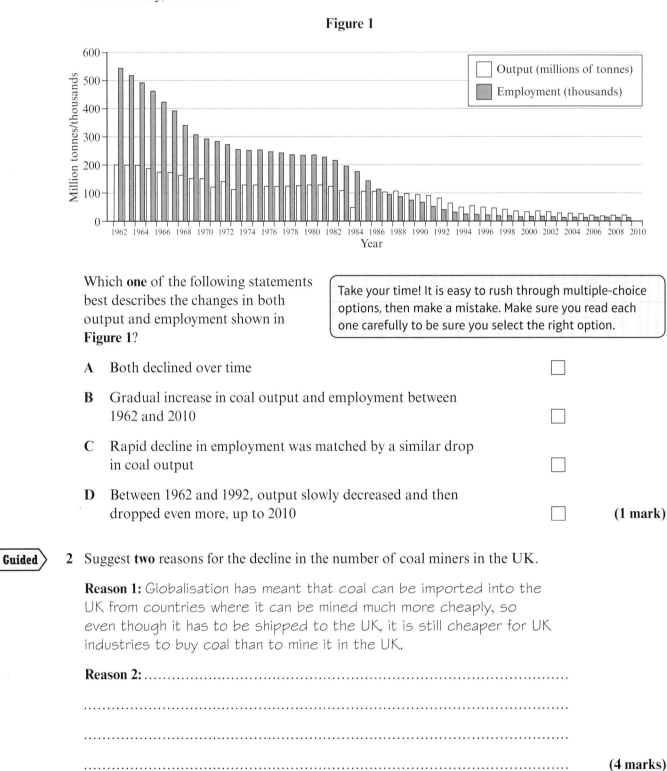

Which **one** of the following statements best describes the changes in both output and employment shown in **Figure 1**?

> Take your time! It is easy to rush through multiple-choice options, then make a mistake. Make sure you read each one carefully to be sure you select the right option.

A Both declined over time ☐

B Gradual increase in coal output and employment between 1962 and 2010 ☐

C Rapid decline in employment was matched by a similar drop in coal output ☐

D Between 1962 and 1992, output slowly decreased and then dropped even more, up to 2010 ☐ **(1 mark)**

⟩ **Guided** ⟩ 2 Suggest **two** reasons for the decline in the number of coal miners in the UK.

Reason 1: Globalisation has meant that coal can be imported into the UK from countries where it can be mined much more cheaply, so even though it has to be shipped to the UK, it is still cheaper for UK industries to buy coal than to mine it in the UK.

Reason 2: ....

....

....

.... **(4 marks)**

UK: post-industrial economy

1   Study **Figure 1**, a table showing changes in the employment structure of the UK between 1973 and 2010.

Figure 1

	1973	1979	1981	1990	2010
Agriculture and fishing	1.9	1.6	1.6	1.4	1.5
Manufacturing	34.7	31.3	28.4	20.5	8.2
Distribution, catering and hotels	17.4	18.4	19.1	21.4	21.3
Banking and finance	6.4	7.2	7.9	15.2	20.3

Percentage of working population employed in each sector, by year

(a) Between which years did manufacturing see the biggest decline?

   A   1973–1979   ☐

   B   1979–1981   ☐

   C   1981–1990   ☐

   D   1990–2010   ☐   **(1 mark)**

> **Guided**

(b) Suggest **one** reason why there has been a shift toward more service sector employment in the UK in recent decades.

One reason is the decline in heavy industry and manufacturing in the UK,

because ....

....

....   **(2 marks)**

2   'Modern industry has the potential to be environmentally sustainable.' Use evidence to support this statement.

> Use your example of sustainable modern industry to answer this question.

....

....

....

....

....

....

....

....

....

....

....   **(6 marks)**

UK: rural change

1   Study **Figure 1**, which provides information about Herefordshire and the UK context, based on 2012 figures.

Figure 1

- Herefordshire is a predominantly rural area.
- The average wage in England is £21 560 per year.
- The average wage in urban areas of England is £23 560 per year.
- The average wage in Herefordshire is £16 398.

> **Guided**

(a)   Explain how the information in **Figure 1** could help account for rural depopulation in Herefordshire.

The average wage in Herefordshire is over £5100 less per year than

the average wage for England, and over £7100 less per year than the

average wage in urban areas of England. This is important for

understanding rural depopulation because ....

....

....   **(2 marks)**

(b)   Study **Figure 2**, a list of other factors which may increase depopulation in remote rural areas.

Figure 2

- Lack of affordable housing to buy or rent.
- Lack of broadband access or mobile phone coverage.
- Very little help for parents with young children.

Choose **two** of the factors listed in **Figure 2**. Explain why each of your chosen factors may increase rural depopulation.

> For each factor, you should make one developed point **or** two points without development.

Factor 1:...

....

....

....

Factor 2:...

....

....

....   **(4 marks)**

UK: developments

1 Study **Figure 1**, a graph showing the projected economic output, per person,
   of the UK's regions for the period 2017–2019.

Figure 1

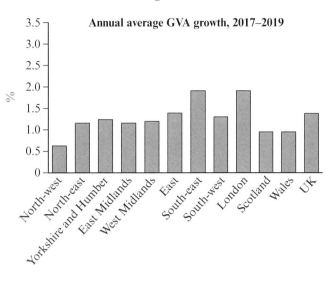

Annual average GVA growth, 2017–2019

Guided

(a) Identify **one** way in which this graph supports the idea of a North–South
     divide in the UK.

The top three regions for economic output per person are all ....

....

.... **(1 mark)**

(b) Suggest **two** reasons why London and the south-east are economically more
     productive than the rest of the UK.

> Reasons for London's strong economic performance are connected to its role as a world-leading finance
> centre. What other reasons do you know of that explain why people earn more, and create more wealth,
> in London and the south-east?

Reason 1: ....

....

....

....

Reason 2: ....

....

....

.... **(4 marks)**

UK and the wider world

1 Study **Figure 1**, a graph showing Foreign Direct Investment (FDI) in the UK between 2010 and 2014.

Figure 1

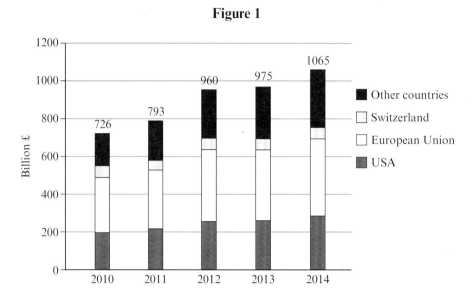

(a) According to **Figure 1**, which **one** of the four following countries or groups of countries had the largest Foreign Direct Investment (FDI) in 2014?

    A Switzerland   ☐

    B Spain   ☐

    C European Union   ☐

    D USA   ☐   **(1 mark)**

(b) What is the percentage increase in FDI in the UK between 2010 and 2014, as shown in **Figure 1**? Give your answer to 1 decimal place.

> To calculate the percentage increase, find the difference between the numbers you are comparing, then divide the difference by the original figure (the 2010 figure) and multiply by 100.

.... **(1 mark)**

⟩ **Guided** ⟩ (c) Explain **one** advantage and **one** disadvantage for the UK of economic links with the European Union.

> All countries need to trade with one another but each country or trading bloc wants to get the best deal for their citizens; for example, by making their trading partners agree to sell at lower prices.

Advantage: The European Union is the world's biggest single market and a very important market for UK products: in 2016, around 45 per cent of the UK's trade was with the EU.

Disadvantage: ....

....

....

.... **(4 marks)**

Essential resources

1 Study **Figure 1**, a diagram showing the average consumption of resources per person per day in six global regions.

Figure 1

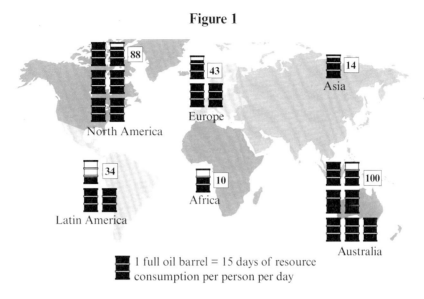

88 North America

43 Europe

14 Asia

34 Latin America

10 Africa

100 Australia

🛢 1 full oil barrel = 15 days of resource consumption per person per day

(a) If the amounts used by each of the six areas are put in numerical order, what will the median number be?

> Make sure you know how to calculate the median number. If there is an odd number of items, the median is the middle number. Here there is an even number so the median is the mean of the two middle numbers (the mean is found by adding the numbers and dividing by how many numbers there are).

10, 14, 34, 43, 88, 100   M = 38.5   **(1 mark)**

> **Guided**

(b) Describe the connection between development and resource consumption.

Consumption increases with development. As economies become more developed they are able to exploit the resources that they already have as well as importing more resources due to the increase in wealth. This means that they use more resources (food, energy, water) as they can afford it.   **(2 marks)**

(c) Explain **one** difference between economic wellbeing and social wellbeing.

> Questions about data presentation can come up on any part of the exam papers.

Economic wellbeing concerns people's jobs or salaries whereas social wellbeing concerns peoples health and everyday life.   **(2 marks)**

UK food resources

7/8

1 Study **Figure 1**, a graph showing the UK's trade with the rest of the world in fresh fruit (total exports of fresh fruit from the UK and total imports of fresh fruit into the UK) and **Figure 2**, a chart showing the main countries from which the UK imports fresh fruit.

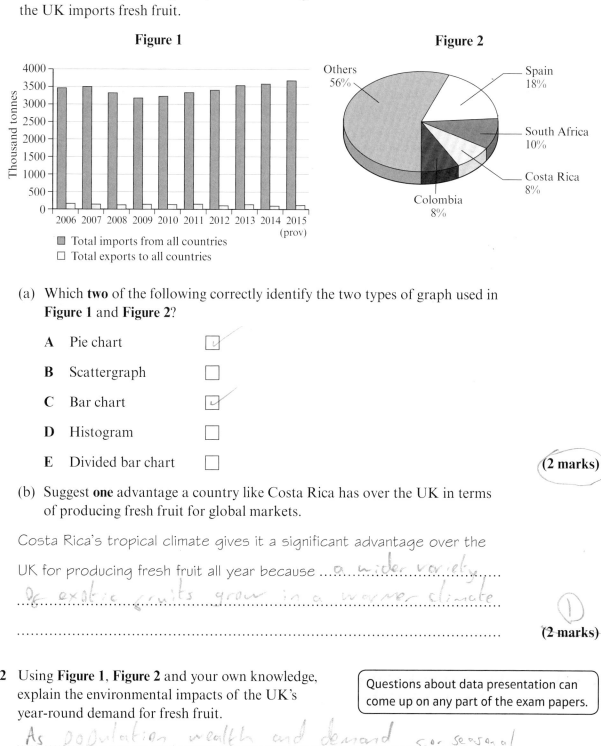

Figure 1

Thousand tonnes

■ Total imports from all countries
☐ Total exports to all countries

Figure 2

Others 56%
Spain 18%
South Africa 10%
Costa Rica 8%
Colombia 8%

(a) Which **two** of the following correctly identify the two types of graph used in **Figure 1** and **Figure 2**?

A Pie chart   ☑

B Scattergraph   ☐

C Bar chart   ☑

D Histogram   ☐

E Divided bar chart ☐   **(2 marks)**

Guided

(b) Suggest **one** advantage a country like Costa Rica has over the UK in terms of producing fresh fruit for global markets.

Costa Rica's tropical climate gives it a significant advantage over the

UK for producing fresh fruit all year because ....a wider variety....

...of exotic fruits grow in a warmer climate........

.... **(2 marks)**

2 Using **Figure 1**, **Figure 2** and your own knowledge, explain the environmental impacts of the UK's year-round demand for fresh fruit.

> Questions about data presentation can come up on any part of the exam papers.

As population wealth and demand for seasonal
products increases the UK has to import more
fresh fruit from other countries because
more people demand a wider variety. Food
transportation will increase the UK's carbon   **(4 marks)**
emissions and carbon footprint as the food
miles increase. This will contribute to climate change.

Had a go ☐   Nearly there ☑   Nailed it! ☐

3/5

UK water resources

1 Study **Figure 1**, a map showing major existing water transfer schemes in England and Wales, and suggested new transfer schemes.

Figure 1

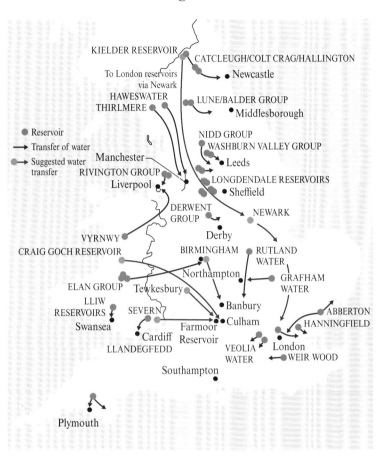

(a) According to **Figure 1**, which **one** of the following regions of England and Wales has the most reservoirs?

A   The south west ☐   C   East Anglia ☐

B   Wales ☐   D   The north ☑ ✓ **(1 mark)**

Guided

(b) Outline **two** reasons why the suggested new water transfer schemes are mainly transferring water from the north and west of the country to the south (the Thames drainage basin).

Reason 1: In the UK, precipitation is much higher in the north and west than in the south and east, so there is usually water surplus in the north and west, while the south and east can experience water deficit.

Reason 2: Population density is higher in Eastern and Southern parts of the UK so more people need more water. **(2 marks)**

(c) Explain **one** disadvantage of using large-scale water transfer schemes to maintain water supplies in the UK.

> Whenever a question asks about advantages or disadvantages, you can use the categories social, economic and environmental to help you answer.

Not all areas might want to transfer water and it might be expensive. **(2 marks)**

UK energy resources

$\frac{8}{8}$

1   Study **Figure 1**, a diagram showing the shares of different energy resources that were used to generate the UK's electricity in 2014 and 2015.

Figure 1

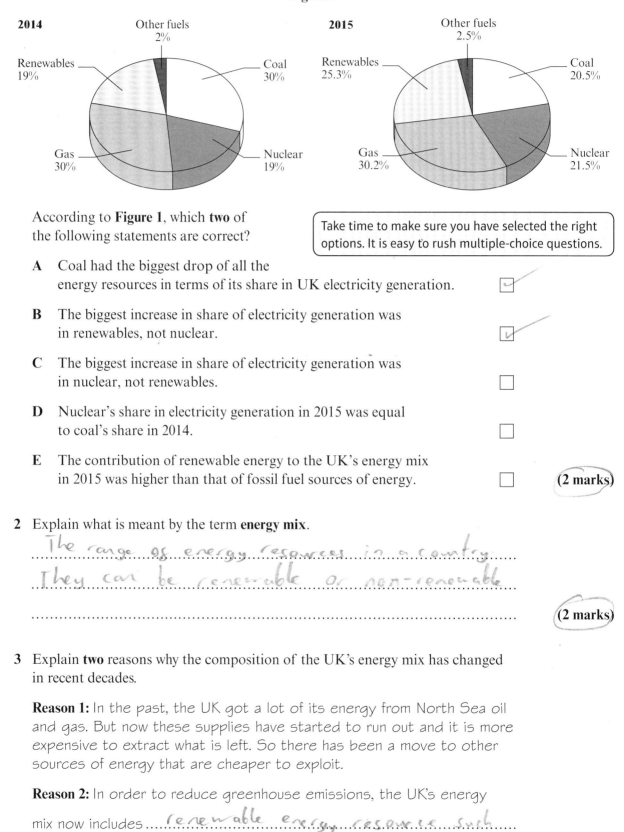

According to **Figure 1**, which **two** of the following statements are correct?

> Take time to make sure you have selected the right options. It is easy to rush multiple-choice questions.

A   Coal had the biggest drop of all the energy resources in terms of its share in UK electricity generation.   ☑

B   The biggest increase in share of electricity generation was in renewables, not nuclear.   ☑

C   The biggest increase in share of electricity generation was in nuclear, not renewables.   ☐

D   Nuclear's share in electricity generation in 2015 was equal to coal's share in 2014.   ☐

E   The contribution of renewable energy to the UK's energy mix in 2015 was higher than that of fossil fuel sources of energy.   ☐   **(2 marks)**

2   Explain what is meant by the term **energy mix**.

The range of energy resources in a country. They can be renewable or non-renewable

(2 marks)

⟩ **Guided** ⟩   3   Explain **two** reasons why the composition of the UK's energy mix has changed in recent decades.

Reason 1: In the past, the UK got a lot of its energy from North Sea oil and gas. But now these supplies have started to run out and it is more expensive to extract what is left. So there has been a move to other sources of energy that are cheaper to exploit.

Reason 2: In order to reduce greenhouse emissions, the UK's energy mix now includes renewable energy resources such as solar power.

(4 marks)

Demand for food

'Food', 'Water' and 'Energy' are options: only revise the one you studied.

1 Study **Figure 1**, a table showing food consumption (in kcal per person per day) in different global regions.

Figure 1

Region	1974–1976	1984–1986	1997–1999	2015
World	2435	2655	2803	2940
Developing countries	2152	2450	2681	2850
Industrialised countries	3065	3206	3380	3440

According to **Figure 1**, which **one** of the following statements is correct?

A   The biggest difference in food consumption per person between 1974 and 2015 occurred in industrialised countries. ☐

B   The world saw a larger increase in food consumption per person between 1974 and 2015 than the increase that occurred in developing countries. ☐

C   The world saw a larger increase in food consumption per person between 1974 and 2015 than the industrialised countries on their own, but this global increase was smaller than the increase for developing countries. ☑

D   The world saw a larger increase in food consumption per person between 1974 and 2015 than the developing countries on their own, but this global increase was smaller than the increase for industrialising countries. ☐   **(1 mark)**

2 Identify **two** factors that affect food supply in a country or region.

> Think about different climates, as well as social and economic situations.

Factor 1: Climate

Factor 2: Conflict   **(2 marks)**

Guided

3 (a) Explain **one** way in which economic development leads to increased food consumption.

When the majority of the population of an LIC farms land to feed themselves (subsistence agriculture), food consumption is low and is mostly made up of one or two plant crops. When people leave rural areas to work in industry in cities, they are able to afford more food.   **(2 marks)**

(b) Explain **one** way in which population growth leads to increased food consumption.

If there are more people more food is needed to feed everyone. It can also raise the demand for a wider variety to increase.   **(2 marks)**

Food insecurity

⟨**Guided**⟩ **1** Study **Figure 1**, which shows some of the impacts of food insecurity.

Figure 1

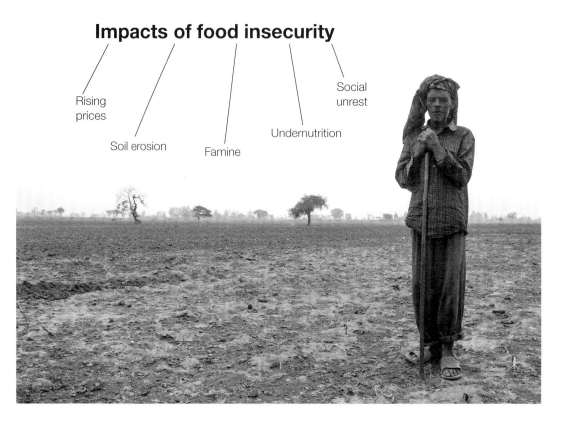

Impacts of food insecurity

Rising prices

Soil erosion

Famine

Undernutrition

Social unrest

Using **Figure 1** and your own knowledge, describe and explain the impacts of food insecurity.

> You can use the prompt words on the image to help you select the impacts you want to explain, but make sure you **explain how** they are the result of food insecurity.

Food insecurity is a lack of reliable access to enough safe, nutritious food.

....

....

....

....

....

....

....

....

....

....

....

.... **(6 marks)**

Named example Increasing food supply

1 Study **Figure 1**, a diagram illustrating two different methods of growing plants without soil.

Figure 1

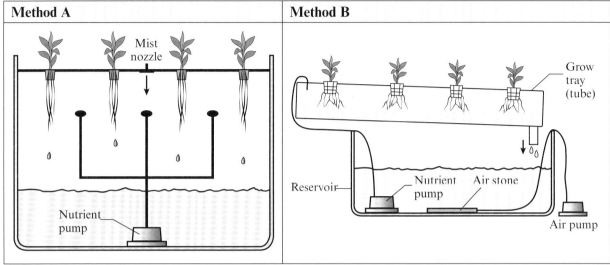

> **Guided**

(a) Identify the **two** methods shown in **Figure 1**.

Method A: Aeroponics   Method B: ....   **(2 marks)**

(b) Explain **one** advantage of growing plants
    without soil as a way of increasing food supply.

> Think about the control that these
> methods give to growers in terms of
> water, nutrients, pests and diseases.

....

....   **(2 marks)**

2 (a) What is meant by the term **appropriate technology**?

....

....   **(1 mark)**

(b) Explain how appropriate technology can be used to increase food supply.

....

....

....

....

....

....

....

....   **(4 marks)**

⊕ Named example Sustainable food supplies

1 (a) Which **one** of the following is the most accurate definition for the term **permaculture**?

   A Growing, processing and delivering food where most people live ☐

   B Only eating fruit and vegetables that are in season ☐

   C Farming that follows the way that natural ecosystems work ☐

   D Using no artificial chemicals in raising livestock: pasture-fed livestock ☐   **(1 mark)**

> **Guided** >

   (b) Explain **one** way in which urban farming can help make food supply more sustainable.

   Growing food in cities reduces the distance that food has to be

   transported to be available to urban populations. This helps make

   food supply more sustainable because ....

   ....   **(2 marks)**

> **Guided** >

   (c) Apart from urban farming initiatives, identify **two** other ways of making food supplies more sustainable.

   First way: Getting meat and fish from sustainable sources

   Second way: ....

   ....   **(2 marks)**

2 Discuss how sustainable food supplies in LICs or NEEs can be increased through local schemes. Use an example in your answer.

   > Make sure you include relevant detail from any example you use.

   ....

   ....

   ....

   ....

   ....

   ....

   ....

   ....

   ....

   ....

   ....

   ....   **(6 marks)**

$\dfrac{7}{8}$

Demand for water

'Water', 'Food' and 'Energy' are options: only revise the one you studied.

1   Study **Figure 1**, a map showing global areas of water deficit and water surplus.

Figure 1

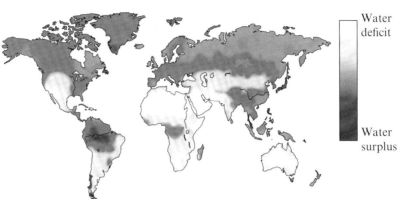

Water deficit

Water surplus

According to **Figure 1**, which **two** of the following statements are correct?

A   All HICs have a water deficit.   ☐

B   Most of Africa has a water deficit.   ☑

C   Australia has a water surplus.   ☐

D   Most of the USA has a water surplus.   ☑

E   Most regions along the Equator have a water surplus.   ☐

F   Most of Europe has a water deficit.   ☐   **(2 marks)**

2   Identify **two** factors that affect water availability in a country or region.

Remember that some of the factors that affect water supply are physical factors relating to geology, climate and so on, while others are human factors that relate to how available water is used (or misused).

Factor 1: Climate - Warmer ℃ = more evaporation.

Factor 2: Geology - Impermeable rock causes water to run into rivers + lakes.   **(2 marks)**

> **Guided**

3   (a)   Explain **one** way in which economic development leads to increased water consumption.

As a country industrialises, water consumption increases significantly

because heavy industry and power generation require water to

cool machinery and to make products   **(2 marks)**

(b)   Explain **one** way in which population growth leads to increased water consumption.

Population growth results in more people that

need water for drinking washing, cleaning

and buying products that use more water.   **(2 marks)**

Water insecurity

> **Guided**

1 Study **Figure 1**, which shows some of the impacts of water insecurity.

Figure 1

Impacts of water insecurity

Waterborne disease

Potential for conflict

Water pollution

Industrial output

Food production

Using **Figure 1** and your own knowledge, describe and explain the impacts of water insecurity.

You can use the prompt words on the image to help you select the impacts you want to explain, but make sure you **explain how** they are the result of water insecurity.

Water security is about people having reliable access to enough safe

water for them to have a healthy and productive life, and about reducing

the risk of water hazards. ....

....

....

....

....

....

....

....

....

....

....   **(6 marks)**

7/8

 Increasing water supply

1 Study **Figure 1**, a diagram showing one strategy for increasing water supply.

Figure 1

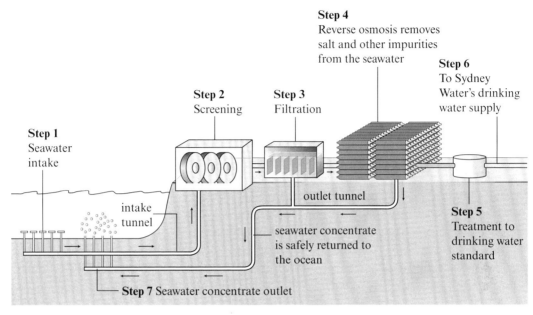

Step 4
Reverse osmosis removes
salt and other impurities
from the seawater

Step 6
To Sydney
Water's drinking
water supply

Step 2
Screening

Step 3
Filtration

Step 1
Seawater
intake

intake
tunnel

outlet tunnel

seawater concentrate
is safely returned to
the ocean

Step 5
Treatment to
drinking water
standard

Step 7 Seawater concentrate outlet

(a) Identify the strategy for increasing water supply shown in **Figure 1**.

...... Desalination .... **(1 mark)**

> **Guided**

(b) Explain **one** advantage of the strategy shown in **Figure 1** as a way of increasing water supply.

Because 97 per cent of the Earth's water is in the sea and therefore

too saline for drinking, growing crops or many other uses, ...So... desalination

removes the salts from the water .... **(2 marks)**

2 (a) Apart from the strategy shown in **Figure 1**, identify **one** other strategy to increase water supply.

...... water transfer schemes. ....

.... **(1 mark)**

(b) Explain **one** advantage and **one** disadvantage of strategies to increase water supply.

> You will have studied a large-scale water transfer scheme to show how its development has had both advantages and disadvantages. You could use information from that to answer this question.

Advantage:...Supplies water from

areas of water surplus to areas of water

deficit.

Disadvantage:...Areas of water surplus may not

want to supply water due to high costs

which causes conflict.

(4 marks)

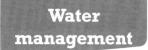

🌐 Named example Sustainable water supplies

1 (a) Which **one** of the following is the most accurate definition for the term **water recycling**?

   A   Artificially recharging aquifers with water
       (e.g. during winter months) ☐

   B   Reusing water that has been used by homes and businesses for
       other purposes, e.g. cooling in industry ☐

   C   Ways to reduce water consumption by using water more
       efficiently and less wastefully ☐

   D   Using no artificial chemicals in cleaning waste water ☐   **(1 mark)**

Guided

   (b) Explain **one** way in which recycling can help make water supply more
       sustainable.

   Recycling water means using 'grey water' (water that has already been

   used for one purpose) to meet other needs – so, for example, water

   used in homes is then recycled for watering grass or as a coolant in

   industry. This helps make water supply more sustainable because ....

   ....

   ....   **(2 marks)**

Guided

   (c) Apart from water recycling, identify **two** other ways of making water
       supplies more sustainable.

   Way 1: Groundwater management

   Way 2: ....   **(2 marks)**

2 Describe and explain how sustainable
   supplies of water in LICs or NEEs can
   be increased through local schemes.
   Use an example in your answer.

> You will have studied an example of a local scheme
> to increase sustainable supplies of water in an LIC
> or an NEE. Use this example in your answer.

   ....

   ....

   ....

   ....

   ....

   ....

   ....

   ....

   ....   **(6 marks)**

Demand for energy

> 'Energy', 'Water' and 'Food' are options: only revise the one you studied.

1   Study **Figure 1**, a graph showing changes in the global consumption of energy, 1990 to 2025 (projected).

Figure 1

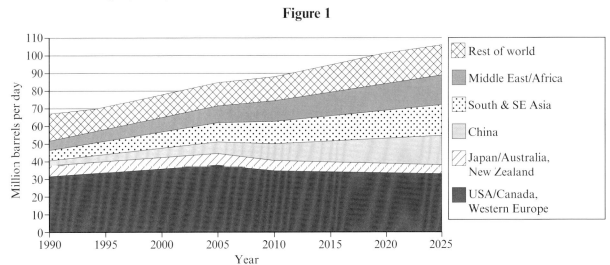

Using **Figure 1**, which **one** of the following statements is correct?

A   Energy consumption in the West (USA/Canada, Western Europe) has increased each year since 2005.   ☐

B   In 2015, South and South East Asia consumed over 70 million barrels (oil equivalent) every day.   ☐

C   The lowest energy use per capita is in China.   ☐

D   By 2025, energy consumption in China is predicted to be approximately 10 times its consumption in 1990.   ☑   **(1 mark)**

2   Identify **two** factors that affect energy supply in a country or region.

Factor 1: .....Economic development.....   Factor 2: .....War + conflict.....   **(2 marks)**

Guided   3   (a)   Explain **one** way in which economic development leads to increased energy consumption.

When the majority of the population are subsistence farmers, energy

consumption is low: people use wood as fuel, and human and animal

muscle power to work their fields. When people leave rural areas to

work in industry in cities, ...energy consumption is.....

.....higher because of money activing increased.....

.....incomes.   **(2 marks)**

(b)   Explain **one** way in which population growth leads to increased energy consumption.

.....More people need more energy. They.....

.....buy appliances that require energy.   **(2 marks)** ①

Energy insecurity

Guided

1 Study **Figure 1**, a diagram showing some impacts of energy insecurity.

Figure 1

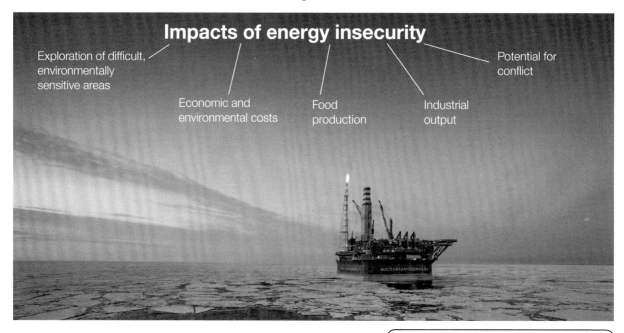

Impacts of energy insecurity

Exploration of difficult, environmentally sensitive areas

Economic and environmental costs

Food production

Industrial output

Potential for conflict

Using **Figure 1** and your own knowledge, describe and explain the impacts of energy insecurity.

> You can use the prompt words on the image to help you select the impacts you want to explain, but make sure you **explain how** they are the result of energy insecurity.

Energy security is about people and industries having reliable

access to enough energy at affordable prices. One impact of energy

insecurity is ....

....

....

....

....

....

....

....

....

....

....

....

....   **(6 marks)**

6
7

 **Increasing energy supply**

1 Study **Figure 1**, a photograph showing one strategy for increasing energy supply.

Figure 1

(a) Identify the strategy for increasing energy supply shown in **Figure 1**.

........Solar energy (renewable)........ **(1 mark)**

> **Guided**

(b) Explain **one** advantage of the strategy shown in **Figure 1** as a way of increasing energy supply.

During daylight hours, around 173 000 terawatts of solar energy

reaches the Earth's surface, ...photovoltaic cells on solar

panels absorb sunlight and produce...........

.......energy............. **(2 marks)**

2 Explain **one** advantage and **one** disadvantage of extracting fossil fuels as a way of increasing energy supply.

> You will have studied an example to show how the extraction of a fossil fuel has both advantages and disadvantages. You could use information from that to answer this question.

Advantage: ......Fossil fuels are a reliable way...... of increasing energy supply as they are efficient and meet up with demands....

Disadvantage: ......Fossil fuels are non-renewable and will eventually deplete. They release carbon emissions when burned which contribute to climate change. **(4 marks)**

🌐 Named example **Sustainable energy supplies**

⟩ **Guided** ⟩   **1** Study **Figure 1**, a photograph of a hydrogen bus in Iceland.

Figure 1

Suggest **one** way in which new technologies, such as the one shown in **Figure 1**, may help to reduce an area's carbon footprint.

Because hydrogen does not emit any CO_2 when used as a fuel, ...

....

....

.... **(2 marks)**

2 Explain **two** benefits of a local renewable energy scheme for communities in LICs or NEEs.

> You will have studied an example of a local renewable energy scheme in an LIC or NEE. You could use this example to add detail to your answer to this question.

Benefit 1: ....

....

....

....

Benefit 2: ....

....

....

.... **(4 marks)**

Working with a resource booklet

This is the type of resource that could be included in a resource booklet for your exam.

Guided

1   Study **Figure 1**, a map showing the location of the Belo Monte hydroelectric
     dam project in Brazil and **Figure 2,** an aerial view of the Bacaja indigenous tribe
     settlement on the banks of the Bacaja River, a tributary of the Xingu River on
     which the Belo Monte dam project is being constructed.

Figure 1   **Figure 2**

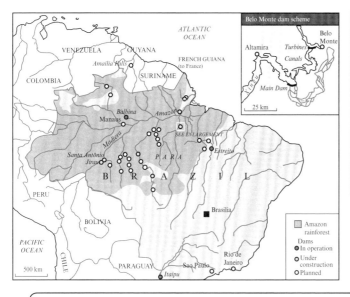

Exam questions will often ask you to refer to the booklet, and could refer to any of the resources in it.

'The development of energy resources in the tropical rainforest creates more
problems than benefits.'

Use **Figure 1**, **Figure 2** and your own understanding to discuss this statement.

The construction of a hydroelectric dam project creates
benefits because HEP produces cheap electricity with low
carbon emissions. Other benefits include

Continue your answer on your
own paper. You should aim to
write about half a side of A4.

....

....

....

....

....

....

....   **(6 marks)**

As you prepare for Paper 3, it is a good idea to summarise what each resource in the booklet shows. Your
notes will help you become familiar with all the resources and give you ideas on how you can use them
in the exam. However, you won't know what the questions will be until the exam itself.

Contemporary geographical issues

> The resource booklet will contain different types of resource, including some that provide background information on an issue and some that set out different points of view, like the ones below.

Guided

1   Study **Figure 1**, the background to the Belo Monte dam project, and **Figure 2**, conflicting views about the Belo Monte project.

Figure 1

The issue

Brazil is an emerging country which has experienced rapid economic growth in recent years. A reliable, secure and sustainable energy supply will be crucial to Brazil's future development. Brazil has a range of energy resources:

- it produces bioelectricity from sugarcane crops
- large deposits of oil and gas have recently been discovered offshore
- there is large potential for wind and solar power
- there is potential for shale gas
- it is a large producer of HEP.

Choices now need to be made about how to expand its electricity supply.

Background to the issue

- Belo Monte, on the Xingu River, is the largest dam currently under construction in the world.
- Its final expected capacity will make it the world's third largest HEP producer.
- It will cost US$14.4 billion.
- 1500 km^2 of Brazilian forest will be destroyed.
- Over 40 000 people will be forced to move away from the area.
- The Xingu River basin is home to 25 000 indigenous people from 40 ethnic groups.
- Several rare and endangered fish species are threatened by the dam.

Figure 2 Conflicting views about the project

Brazilian government	Hydroelectric power is clean, green energy and we have the potential to produce high amounts of HEP, which will benefit many millions of people in Brazil.
Celebrity conservationist	The Amazon rainforest is a global resource and should be protected for future generations. I am against HEP development.
A migrant worker	I moved from the overcrowded city for a house and a well-paid construction job. I am in favour of HEP development.
An indigenous tribal person	Generations of my family have lived off the river and we may lose the traditions of our tribe. I am against HEP development.

> Not all the questions in Section A of Paper 3 will refer to multiple resources – some will just refer to one. You need to use your own understanding of the issue as well as information from the resource booklet.

Explain **one** way in which deforestation in the Xingu River basin might **benefit** people living in the area, and **one** way in which it might **disadvantage** people in the area.

> Select information from the resources to support points in your answers.

Benefit: Migrant workers would benefit because they would get a job and earn money from working on the construction of the dam.

Disadvantage: ....

....

.... **(4 marks)**

Evaluating issues

1 Study **Figure 1**, which shows three projects that have been suggested for development of the Xingu River basin.

The resource booklet will include a description of three projects relating to an issue featured in the booklet. The question paper will then ask a question involving these three projects.

Figure 1

- **Option 1** Build the Belo Monte dam and further HEP schemes to produce more HEP
- **Option 2** Make the area a national park and increase the amount of energy produced from biogas
- **Option 3** Develop smaller HEP dams, and solar and wind power

Which **one** of the three projects do you think would be the best long-term plan for the development of the Xingu River basin area? Use evidence from resources on **pages 119** and **120** and your own understanding to explain why you have reached this decision.

Your answer must consider all three alternative projects and establish a clear argument about the meaning of the 'best long-term' plan. There is no preferred project, and all projects can be justified.

For a strong answer, you need to include:

- **range** – refer to at least two advantages and two disadvantages (costs/benefits, good/bad, positive/negative impacts) of your chosen project
- **detailed evidence** – make extended explanations using detail from the resources, rather than vague assertions
- **counter-argument** – explain why you have rejected one or more projects, but also consider one of its strengths
- **balance** – refer to both people and/or environment in terms of advantages and disadvantages
- **a synoptic approach** – bring in some knowledge and understanding from the rest of your course
- **an overall judgement** – come to a view that is logically linked to the evidence you have used
- **SPaG** – there are three marks available for spelling, punctuation and grammar and the relevant and appropriate use of specialist vocabulary.

Chosen project: ....

....

....

....

....

....

....

....

(9 marks + 3 marks for SPaG)

Continue your answer on your own paper. You should aim to write between one and two sides of A4.

Enquiry questions

1   Study **Figure 1**, which shows Lulworth Cove in Dorset.

Figure 1

> **Guided**

Suggest **one** reason why the location shown in **Figure 1** would be suitable for an enquiry into tourism at coastal locations.

The car park is full so there would be plenty of visitors to ....

....

....   **(2 marks)**

2   State the title of your own fieldwork enquiry in which **human** geography data were collected.

Title of fieldwork enquiry:...

....

Explain **two** advantages of the location(s) used for your fieldwork enquiry.

> For this question you need to identify **two** advantages of your location(s) **and** explain why **each** was an advantage in terms of the aim of your enquiry.

Advantage 1:..

....

....

....

Advantage 2:..

....

....

....   **(4 marks)**

Selecting, measuring and recording data

1   Study **Figure 1**, a photograph showing part of a coastal location and **Figure 2**,
    a photograph showing part of an urban location.

Figure 1   **Figure 2**

Identify **two** data collection techniques that could be
used to carry out a geographical fieldwork investigation
in **one** of the areas shown (in **Figure 1** or **Figure 2**).

> **Identify** is similar to **state**. You do
> not need to add a description or
> explanation.

Area chosen: ....

Technique 1: ....

....

Technique 2: ....

.... **(2 marks)**

2   Justify **one** primary data collection method used in relation to the aim(s) of your
    own **human** geography enquiry.

> **Justify** means you need to support a case for your answer with evidence. For this answer, you should
> identify one primary data collection method that you used and explain why it was appropriate for your
> enquiry (for example, how accurate the data was, how well it fitted with the aims of your enquiry), etc.

Primary data collection method: ....

....

....

....

....

.... **(3 marks)**

Processing and presenting data

1   Study **Figure 1**, a table presenting data collected by students conducting a river study in the Vale of Edale area.

Figure 1

Distance from water's edge	Site 1 width = 127 cm			Site 2 width = 89 cm		
	Depth (cm)	Pebble length (cm)	Pebble roundness	Depth (cm)	Pebble length (cm)	Pebble roundness
0	0	0	0	0	0	0
25 cm	8	15	angular	23	22	angular
50 cm	19	27	very angular	87	27	angular
75 cm	45	45	sub-angular	73	65	sub-angular
100 cm	38	12	angular			
125 cm	11	8	angular			

Suggest **one** appropriate data presentation technique a student could use to present the channel width and depth measurements.

.... **(1 mark)**

2   Study **Figure 2**, a table presenting the replies to a questionnaire about the quality of an urban environment.

Figure 2

Question: Is litter a problem in Fernham ward?	Age group (years)	Number of replies Yes	Number of replies No
	0–4	0	0
	5–14	2	1
	15–24	6	0
	25–64	7	18
	over 65	3	0

(a)   A student planned to construct a scattergraph to present the data shown in **Figure 2**.

Suggest **one** reason why a scattergraph is an inappropriate method to show this data.

> You should be able to explain the advantages and disadvantages of a number of data presentation methods.

....

.... **(2 marks)**

Guided

(b)   Suggest a graphing method to use that would be more appropriate to show this data.

A histogram, because each bar of a histogram is used for a ....

....

.... **(2 marks)**

Analysing data and reaching conclusions

1 State the title of your own fieldwork enquiry in which **physical** geography data were collected.

Title of fieldwork enquiry: ....

....

Assess how effective your analysis of your **physical** geography data was in helping you reach a reliable conclusion.

> **Assess** means 'make an informed judgement'.

> This question looks challenging but it is basically asking you to use what you know about your own physical geography fieldwork analysis to answer a question.
>
> So first, note down the analysis you did for physical fieldwork: the methods you used to understand what your data was showing you (such as calculations). Your analysis helped you **describe** your data and **explain** its relationship to geographical theories. Your analysis also showed you whether your data did **not** fit with expectations.
>
> Like all aspects of fieldwork, different analysis techniques have both strengths and limitations, and these are what you need to consider when thinking about the reliability of your conclusions. **Do not worry about saying that you think your analysis could have been improved: this is exactly what is meant by 'how effective'.**

....

....

....

....

....

....

....

....

....

....

....

.... **(6 marks)**

Evaluating geographical enquiries

1 Study **Figure 1**, which shows evaluations from five students who carried out fieldwork on the River Dee in North Wales.

Figure 1

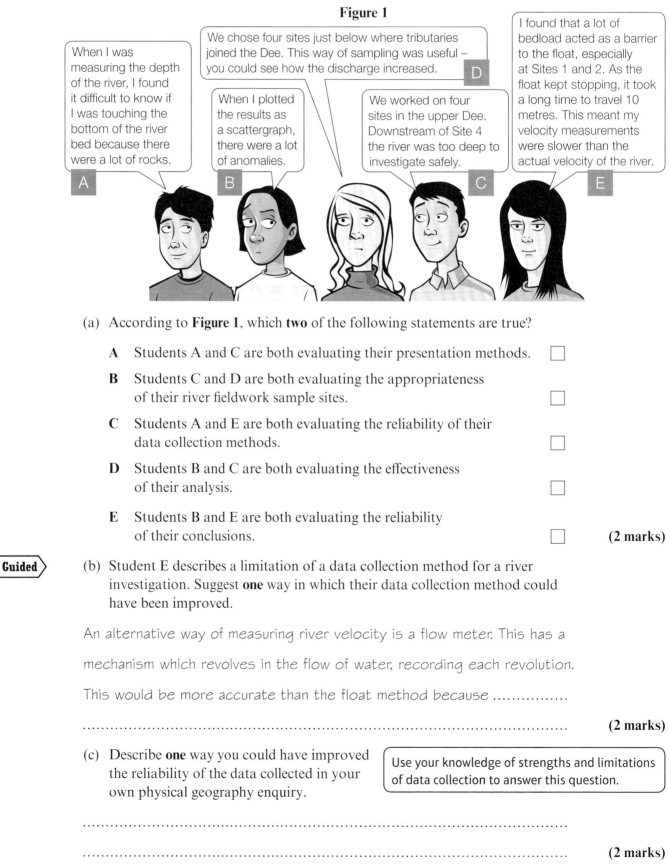

(a) According to **Figure 1**, which **two** of the following statements are true?

    A   Students A and C are both evaluating their presentation methods. ☐

    B   Students C and D are both evaluating the appropriateness of their river fieldwork sample sites. ☐

    C   Students A and E are both evaluating the reliability of their data collection methods. ☐

    D   Students B and C are both evaluating the effectiveness of their analysis. ☐

    E   Students B and E are both evaluating the reliability of their conclusions. ☐ **(2 marks)**

Guided

(b) Student E describes a limitation of a data collection method for a river investigation. Suggest **one** way in which their data collection method could have been improved.

An alternative way of measuring river velocity is a flow meter. This has a

mechanism which revolves in the flow of water, recording each revolution.

This would be more accurate than the float method because ....

.... **(2 marks)**

(c) Describe **one** way you could have improved the reliability of the data collected in your own physical geography enquiry.

> Use your knowledge of strengths and limitations of data collection to answer this question.

....

.... **(2 marks)**

6-mark questions

> **Guided**

1 Study **Figure 1**, which shows a 6-mark exam-style question, and the sample answer that follows it.

Figure 1

Storm Desmond's devastating trail of destruction

A family and their dog were rescued by the Coastguard on Warwick Road in the centre of Carlisle after heavy rain and strong winds from Storm Desmond tore through Britain, killing one person.

The Environment Agency declared 130 flood warnings, while residents in parts of Cumbria were evacuated from their homes. Bridges collapsed, rivers burst their banks and landslides were triggered as torrential rain swept through large swathes of the north of England and Scotland.

Adrian Holme, from Cumbria Fire and Rescue Service, told the BBC the flood is "unprecedented" and "exceptionally challenging". He said it was "absolutely devastating", adding: "The flood defences that were built here in 2012 haven't been breached, they have been over-topped. We have had 24 hours of constant rain."

He added: "This is absolutely devastating for the town of Keswick. As you can see behind us, the water is huge and there are hundreds of properties that have been devastated and flooded. And some of these people have been flooded three times, our hearts must go out to them."

Walesonline.co.uk, 6 December 2015

'Weather is becoming more extreme in the UK.' Use evidence from **Figure 1** and your own knowledge to support this statement.

In 6-mark questions, 2 marks are available for AO1 and 4 marks are for AO2:

- AO1 is about showing your knowledge – so, for example, you could use your knowledge to explain what is meant by extreme weather, or to show that you knew Storm Desmond set a new rainfall record for two consecutive days of rain in Cumbria

- AO2 is about showing your geographical understanding – in this case, AO2 marks would be available for using evidence from Figure 1 to support your answer about weather becoming more extreme.

Extreme weather is when weather conditions are significantly different from the average weather patterns. If weather is becoming more extreme in the UK, this would mean not only that individual weather events are extreme, but that there is an increasing number of these extreme events. ....

....

....

....

....

.... **(6 marks)**

Continue your answer on your own paper. You should aim to write about half a side of A4.

9-mark questions

> **Guided**

1 Study this 9-mark exam-style question and the sample answer that follows it.

'Economic development only has positive effects on quality of life for people in LICs and NEEs.'

Do you agree with this statement?

Yes ☐   No ☐

Justify your decision.

In 9-mark questions, there are marks for three assessment objectives: AO1, AO2 and AO3:

- AO1 is about showing your **knowledge**. There is a maximum of 3 marks available for AO1. In the case of this question, you could gain AO1 marks by adding detailed knowledge about the effects of economic development.

- AO2 is about showing your geographical **understanding**. There is a maximum of 3 marks available for AO2. For this question, you would be showing your accurate geographical understanding of the positive and negative effects of economic development on quality of life for people in LICs and/or NEEs.

- AO3 is about **applying** your knowledge and understanding in the way that you evaluate the two sides of the argument in this question (that economic development does only have positive effects versus that economic development can have effects that are not positive) in order to justify your decision. There is a maximum of 3 marks available for AO3.

- There are no right answers to the question: you can argue either side, but you need to **justify** the decision you make.

Economic development does have many positive effects on quality

of life for people in LICs and NEEs. Quality of life in rural settlements

is very low: people work very hard for very little money, there are

few services and low levels of education and healthcare. This is why

rural–urban migration is so high in LICs and NEEs. ....

....

....

....

....

....

....

....

....

....

....

....   **(9 marks)**

Continue your answer on your own paper. You should aim to write one to two sides of A4.

Paper 3

1 Study the following extract from a Paper 3 mark scheme. The marks have been removed.

Level	Marks	Description
3 (Detailed)		AO3 Demonstrates thorough application of knowledge and understanding in evaluating the effectiveness of the chosen project in terms of socio-economic and environmental benefits.
		AO3 Applies knowledge and understanding to make a decision based on a wide range of supportive evidence, making detailed links between content from different areas of the course of study.
		AO4 Communicates findings with clarity.

Which **one** of the following extended writing questions do you think this mark scheme applies to?

A   Paper 3 Section A Issue evaluation: 6-mark data response question   ☐

B   Paper 3 Section A Issue evaluation: 9-mark decision-making question   ☐

C   Paper 3 Section B Fieldwork: 6-mark 'assess' question   ☐

D   Paper 3 Section B Fieldwork: 9-mark 'to what extent' question   ☐

E   Paper 3 3-mark SPaG question   ☐   **(1 mark)**

2 Study the following extract from a Paper 3 mark scheme. The marks have been removed.

Level	Marks	Description
3 (Detailed)		AO3 Provides detailed evaluation of results.
		AO3 Evaluates contribution made by results to the conclusion(s) reached in detail.
		AO3 Provides an informed judgement as to the extent to which the results contributed to reaching a reliable conclusion.

Which **one** of the following extended writing questions do you think this mark scheme applies to?

A   Paper 3 Section B Fieldwork: 6-mark 'assess' question on data presentation   ☐

B   Paper 3 Section B Fieldwork: 9-mark 'to what extent' question on reliability   ☐

C   Paper 3 Section B Fieldwork: 9-mark 'to what extent' question on accuracy   ☐   **(1 mark)**

3 Which **one** of the following provides the correct definition for Assessment Objective 3 (AO3)?

A   Apply knowledge and understanding to interpret, analyse and evaluate geographical information and issues to make judgements   ☐

B   Select, adapt and use a variety of skills and techniques to investigate questions and issues and communicate findings   ☐

C   Demonstrate geographical understanding of concepts and how they are used in relation to places, environments and processes; the interrelationships between places, environments and processes   ☐

D   Demonstrate knowledge of locations, places, processes, environments and different scales   ☐   **(1 mark)**

Had a go ☐ Nearly there ☐ Nailed it! ☐

Atlas and map skills

In the exam, there will not be a separate section testing your geographical, mathematics and statistics skills. Instead, you might need to use these skills in any of the three exam papers, when answering questions about the topics you have studied.

The questions on **pages 130** to **142** are designed to help you practise these skills. Not all of the questions are in the style of the questions you will find in the exam.

1 Study **Figure 1**, a map showing global distribution of countries according to levels of income, and **Figure 2**, a table giving data on GNI per person for selected countries for 2011.

Figure 1

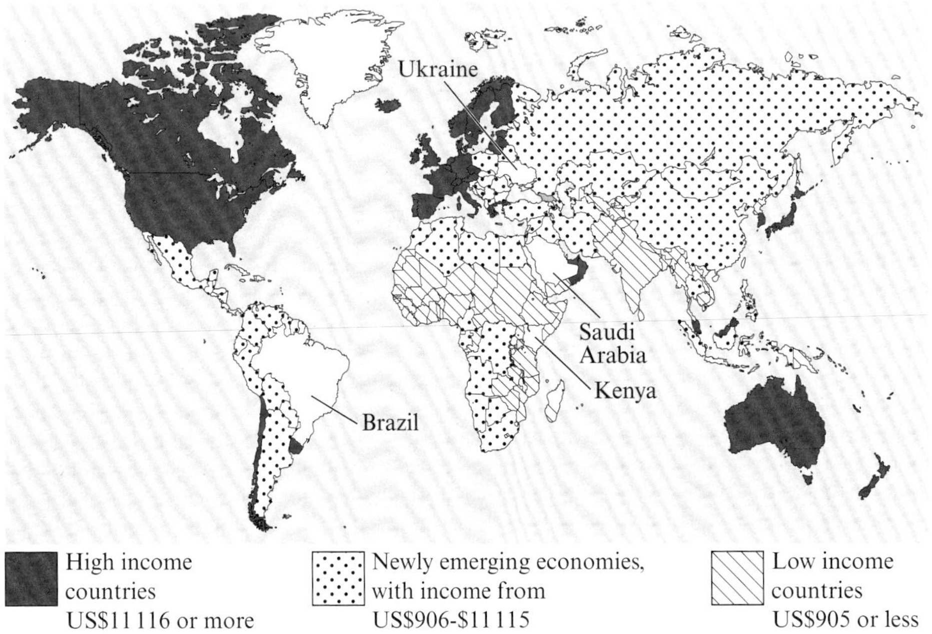

Ukraine
Saudi Arabia
Kenya
Brazil
High income countries US$11 116 or more
Newly emerging economies, with income from US$906-$11 115
Low income countries US$905 or less

Figure 2

Country	Brazil	Kenya	Saudi Arabia	Ukraine
GNI per person (US$)	$14 301	$2590	$49 940	$8170

(a) Complete **Figure 1** by shading in Brazil, Kenya, Saudi Arabia and Ukraine according to the data in **Figure 2**.

Your shading doesn't need to be perfect – just clear and accurate.

(2 marks)

(b) Which **one** of the following identifies the type of map used in **Figure 1**?

A Isoline ☐

B Topological ☐

C Proportional symbol ☐

D Choropleth ☐

(1 mark)

Guided

(c) Using evidence from **Figure 1**, describe the global distribution of levels of income.

The highest income countries can be found in the continents of ....

....

.... **(2 marks)**

Types of map and scale

> **Guided**

1 Study **Figure 1**, a map showing the global distribution of three ecosystems.

Figure 1

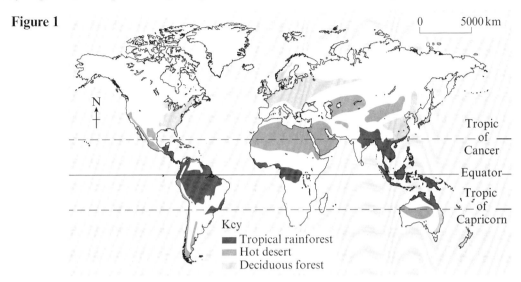

Describe the location of hot desert ecosystems shown in **Figure 1**.

> Here you can use latitude, hemispheres, continent names and compass directions in your description.

Most hot deserts occur close to the Tropics of Cancer and Capricorn.

The greatest extent of hot desert is in ....

.... **(2 marks)**

2 Study **Figure 2**, Mappleton in 1910, and **Figure 3**, Mappleton in 1990.

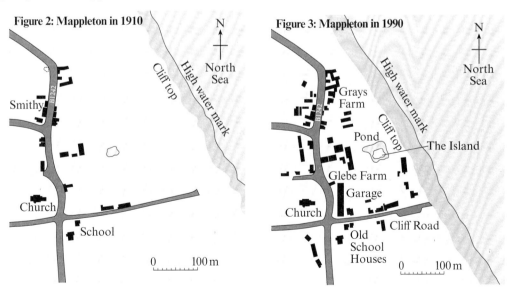

(a) Calculate how many metres the cliff top receded towards Mappleton between 1910 and 1990.

.... **(1 mark)**

(b) Calculate how far in metres the church was from the high-water mark in 1990.

.... **(1 mark)**

Grid references and distances

1 Study **Figure 1**, a map extract.

Figure 1

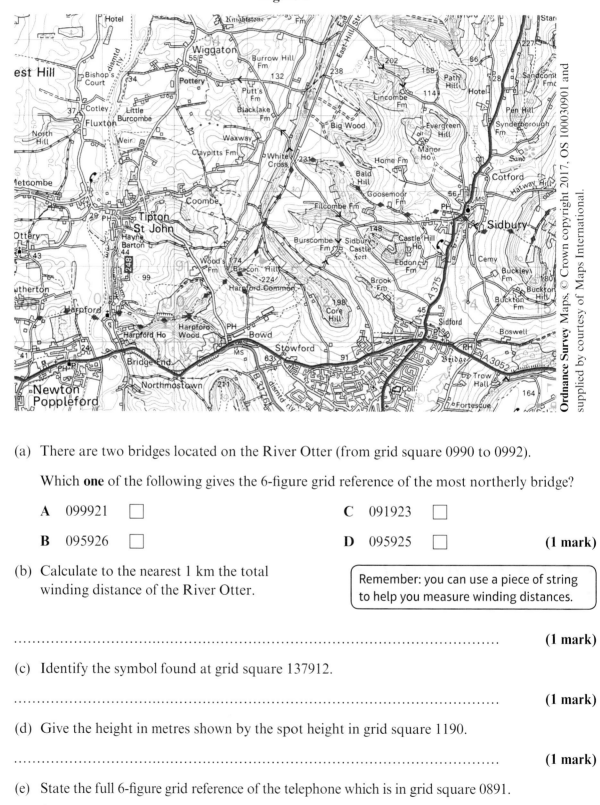

Ordnance Survey Maps. © Crown copyright 2017, OS 100030901 and supplied by courtesy of Maps International.

(a) There are two bridges located on the River Otter (from grid square 0990 to 0992).

Which **one** of the following gives the 6-figure grid reference of the most northerly bridge?

A 099921 ☐   **C** 091923 ☐

B 095926 ☐   **D** 095925 ☐   **(1 mark)**

(b) Calculate to the nearest 1 km the total winding distance of the River Otter.

> Remember: you can use a piece of string to help you measure winding distances.

.... **(1 mark)**

(c) Identify the symbol found at grid square 137912.

.... **(1 mark)**

(d) Give the height in metres shown by the spot height in grid square 1190.

.... **(1 mark)**

(e) State the full 6-figure grid reference of the telephone which is in grid square 0891.

.... **(1 mark)**

Cross sections and relief

Guided 1 Draw lines to match the following contour patterns (aerial view) to the cross-sectional shape of the land.

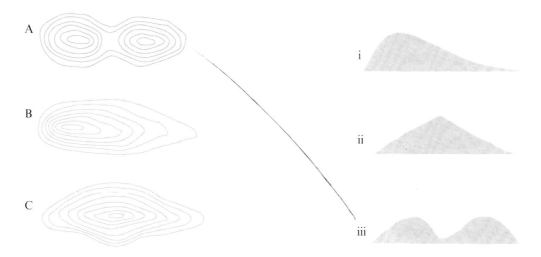

(2 marks)

2 Use **Figure 1** on **page 132** to help you answer the following question.

Complete the sentences by using the words in the box below.

flat	steep	99 m	199 m	flatter	steeper	40 m	70 m

The land to the east of the River Otter is .... It rises to a

maximum height of .... above sea level. In comparison,

the land to the west of the river is .... and rises to a height of

approximately .... above sea level.   (2 marks)

3 Draw a cross-sectional diagram of the contour pattern below.

As each contour crosses the A–B line, put a tick mark on the x-axis.

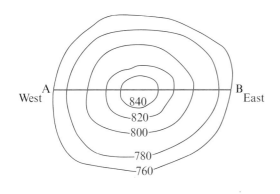

(2 marks)

Physical and human patterns

1   Study **Figure 1,** a map extract showing the town of Alnwick.

Figure 1

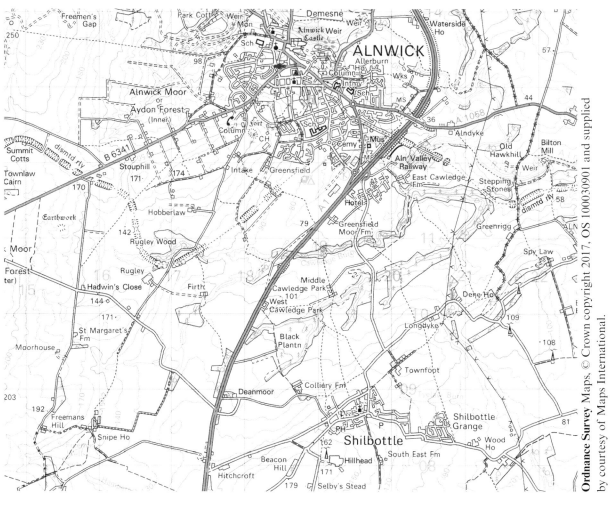

Ordnance Survey Maps, © Crown copyright 2017, OS 100030901 and supplied by courtesy of Maps International.

(a)   Describe the shape of the settlement of Alnwick in **Figure 1**. Use map evidence in your answer.

Alnwick has a nucleated settlement shape because ....

....

....

....   **(2 marks)**

(b)   Suggest **one** reason why Alnwick will have difficulty expanding. Use map evidence in your answer.

> Look at how the land is being used close to the edges of the settlement, on the rural–urban fringe. How might this hinder the expansion of Alnwick?

....

....

....

....   **(2 marks)**

Human activity and OS maps

1 Use **Figure 1** on **page 134** to help you answer the following questions.

(a) State **one** piece of map evidence in grid square 1912 that would be an important facility for local residents.

    ....

    .... **(1 mark)**

(b) Suggest **one** form of public transport that can be used in grid square 1813.

> Remember that public transport includes trains, buses and trams.

    ....

    .... **(1 mark)**

(c) Shilbottle is a village to the south east of Alnwick. Identify **two** pieces of map evidence confirming that it is a village.

> Villages will have three common services. Think about village services that are often at risk of being closed down.

    ....

    ....

    ....

    .... **(2 marks)**

⟩ **Guided** ⟩ (d) 'Shilbottle is a rural settlement.' Using map evidence, justify this statement.

Shilbottle is surrounded by a rural landscape. The many farms around

the area help prove this. For example, South East Farm is located to

the south east of Shilbottle. The map also shows ....

    ....

    ....

    ....

    ....

    ....

    .... **(4 marks)**

Sketch maps and annotations

1 Study **Figure 1**, a field sketch of a meander on the River Rudd.

Figure 1

(a) Which **one** of the following gives three correct labels for the sketch map in **Figure 1**?

> With questions like this, look for labels you know to be incorrect and eliminate those options first.

    A   A = marshland, C = slow-flowing water, D = fast-flowing water   ☐

    B   B = river cliff, C = slow-flowing water, D = fast-flowing water   ☐

    C   B = river cliff, C = fast-flowing water, D = slow-flowing water   ☐

    D   A = woodland, C = river cliff, D = slow-flowing water   ☐   **(1 mark)**

> **Guided**

(b) Add an annotation for 'river cliff' in the space below.

A river cliff is the steep-sided bank of the river which forms when ....

.... **(2 marks)**

2 Study **Figure 2**, an OS map extract of Sherburn.

Draw a sketch map of the settlement in the box. Include these details: the railway line; main roads; the settlement of Sherburn; location of church in GR 3142; Broomside House.

Figure 2

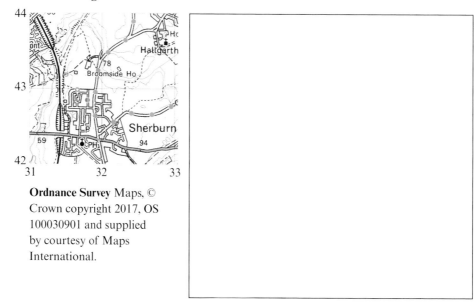

Ordnance Survey Maps, © Crown copyright 2017, OS 100030901 and supplied by courtesy of Maps International.

Using and interpreting images

1   Study **Figure 1**, a photograph of the Hayle Estuary in Cornwall.

Figure 1

(a) Which **one** of the following describes the type of photograph shown in **Figure 1**?

    A   Ground level   **C**   Vertical aerial

    B   Oblique aerial   **D**   Satellite   **(1 mark)**

Guided

(b) State **two** advantages of using a photograph like the one shown in **Figure 1**.

Advantage 1: It is easy to compare different land uses.

Advantage 2: ....

.... **(2 marks)**

2   Study **Figure 2**, an OS map extract of the Hayle Estuary in Cornwall.

Figure 2

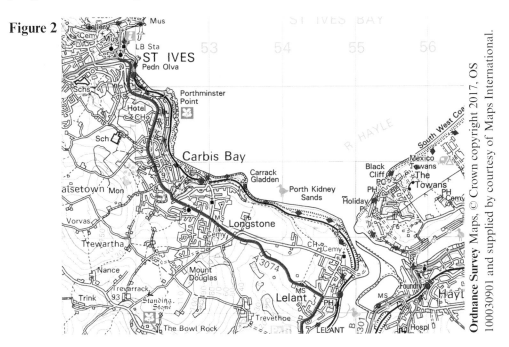

Ordnance Survey Maps. © Crown copyright 2017, OS 100030901 and supplied by courtesy of Maps International.

State **one** piece of information from the map that cannot be seen on the photograph.

> OS maps will always orientate north unless otherwise stated.

.... **(1 mark)**

Graphical skills 1

1   Study **Figure 1**, a graph showing the growth in bicycle use observed (by traffic count) in New York City.

Figure 1

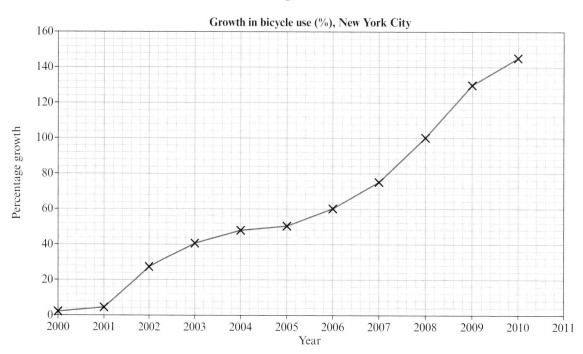

(a)   Complete the graph in **Figure 1** by plotting the 2011 figure of 150 per cent.   **(1 mark)**

> Guided

(b)   Calculate the percentage growth in bicycle use observed between 2006 and 2009.

> When the vertical axis of a graph is already in percentages, you do not need to calculate percentage increase as you do with figures. Here you simply take the 2006 percentage away from the 2009 percentage.

(1 mark)

130 – .... *per cent*

(c)   Calculate how long it took for observed bicycle use to increase by 100 per cent.

> When the vertical axis of a graph is already in percentages, you do not need to calculate an increase by 100 per cent in the way you would when you are dealing with figures (where an increase of 100 per cent means the original number is doubled). Here you need to start by reading off the year when percentage growth reached 100 per cent.

....

....   **(1 mark)**

Graphical skills 2

1 Study **Figure 1**, a graph showing the results of a three-minute traffic survey completed by a GCSE class.

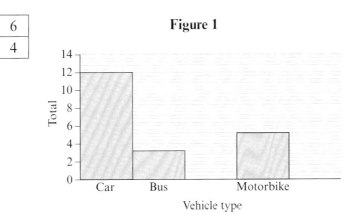

| Lorry | 6 |
| Van | 4 |

Figure 1

(a) Complete the graph in **Figure 1** using the data in the table.   **(2 marks)**

(b) Calculate how many vehicles there were in total.

.... **(1 mark)**

2 Study **Figure 2,** a graph showing the population structure of a country.

Figure 2

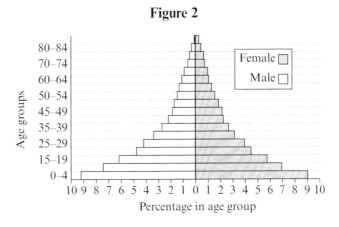

(a) State the correct term for the type of graph shown in **Figure 2**.

.... **(1 mark)**

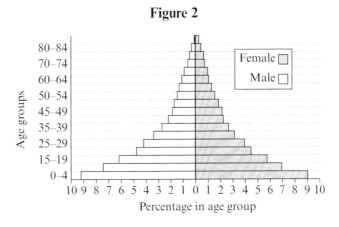
Guided

(b) Describe the population structure shown in this graph.

The country shown has a high ....

....

.... **(2 marks)**

(c) One student decides to present the traffic data in **Figure 1** as a line graph. Suggest **one** reason why this graphical technique is inappropriate for the data collected.

> The difference between **discrete** and **continuous** data is important for answering this question correctly.

....

.... **(2 marks)**

Graphical skills 3

1 Study **Figure 1**, which shows internet users in European countries in 2008.

Figure 1

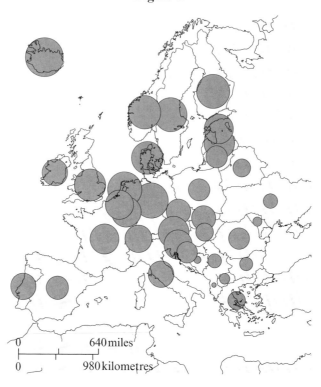

(a) State the correct term for the graphical method shown in **Figure 1**.

> Proportional means that two or more things change at the same rate.

.... **(1 mark)**

> **Guided**

(b) Suggest **one** advantage and **one** disadvantage of using this method to present information.

Advantage: The graphic representation makes initial comparison between data very straightforward.

Disadvantage: ....

....

....

.... **(2 marks)**

2 Which **one** of the following graphical methods would be most appropriate for graphing movement from an origin to a destination?

     A   Desire line map   ☐

     B   Isoline graph   ☐

     C   Dot map   ☐

     D   Dispersion graph   ☐   **(1 mark)**

Numbers and statistics 1

1   Study **Figure 1**, which shows global population data from 2010 to 2015.

Figure 1

	2010	2011	2012	2013	2014	2015
India	1 230 984 504	1 210 193 422	1 263 589 839	1 279 498 874	1 295 291 543	1 311 050 521
World	6 929 725 043					7 349 472 099

(a)   Calculate the percentage of the world's population that lived in India in 2015, according to **Figure 1**.

> Divide India's population value by the world's population value, then multiply the answer by 100.

....   **(1 mark)**

(b)   Calculate India's population percentage increase between 2010 and 2015, according to **Figure 1**.

....   **(1 mark)**

(c)   **Figure 1** shows India's population change from 2010 to 2015. Suggest a type of graph that could best represent this data.

....

....   **(2 marks)**

⟩ **Guided** ⟩   2   Study **Figure 2**, which shows population by rural/urban residence in India, 2011.

Figure 2

Total population:	1 210 193 422
Rural:	833 087 662
Urban:	377 105 760

Calculate and explain the ratio of rural to urban population in 2011, according to **Figure 2**.

833 087 662 ÷ 377 105 760 = ...

This means for every 1 person living in an urban area in India ....

....

....

....   **(2 marks)**

Numbers and statistics 2

1   Study **Figure 1**, which shows peak flow data for the River Douglas at Wigan.

Figure 1

Water year	2004–5	2005–6	2006–7	2007–8	2008–9	2009–10	2010–11
Peak flow m³/s	17.7	10.7	22.9	18.6	23.2	14.8	22.6

(a)   Calculate the mean peak flow over the period shown in **Figure 1**.

....

.... m³/s   **(1 mark)**

(b)   Calculate the median value for peak flow shown in **Figure 1**.

> The **median** is the middle value. First write the values in order from smallest to largest.

....

.... m³/s   **(1 mark)**

(c)   Explain what is meant by the **interquartile range**.

....

....

....   **(2 marks)**

(d)   Calculate the interquartile range for the data shown in **Figure 1**.

> The interquartile range is the difference between the lower and upper quartile values.

....

....   **(1 mark)**

⟩ **Guided** ⟩   (e)   Suggest **one** way in which the data from **Figure 1** could be used.

The discharge data could be used by authorities involved in the

management of ....

....   **(2 marks)**

Answers

Where an example answer is given, this is not necessarily the only correct response. In most cases there is a range of responses that can gain full marks.

1. Natural hazards
1 **A** An event that has threatened life and property
2 Tectonic
3 If the human population significantly increased this could increase congestion on the roads along the evacuation routes. This would increase the risk of the hazard because more people would be in danger if an eruption impacted on the area along the evacuation route.

2. Plate tectonics theory
1 **D** Core
2 *Example* Continental crust is normally made of granite, whereas oceanic is normally basaltic. *Other differences include density (oceanic crust is denser) and age (oceanic crust is younger) – plus continental crust has continents on it.*
3 As heat rises from the core as a result of radioactive decay, it releases convection currents in the form of cells. These currents are believed to be strong enough to move tectonic plates.

3 Plate margin processes
1 Volcanoes are found in lines (linear distribution). The distribution is mostly associated with the main plate margins around the Pacific Ocean, known as the Pacific Ring of Fire.
2 Any one of the following:
- **Destructive margin** Plates push together and the oceanic plate is subducted beneath the continental plate. Energy is released as earthquakes. Rising magma (oceanic) can create volcanoes on the continental crust side.
- **Constructive margin** Plates are forced apart by basaltic material, which creates new crust. As the crust is pulled apart, it creates fissures and faults where molten magma can reach the surface, forming volcanoes.
- **Conservative margin** Plates slide past one another causing earthquakes because of friction. Because there is no plate being created or destroyed, there is no magma rising to the surface and therefore no volcanoes.
- **Collision margin** Continental plates are pushed together, buckling the crust and creating fold mountains. Earthquakes can occur here.
3 Destructive plate margins are where oceanic and continental plates meet and the oceanic plate subducts under the continental one. The collision of the plates buckles the continental plate. The friction is great, so pressure builds and is suddenly released, giving off large amounts of energy as seismic waves, which causes earthquakes. These can often be shallow. Earthquakes of up to magnitude 9.0 can occur and sometimes tsunamis, as in Japan in 2011.

4. Tectonic hazards: effects
1 Primary effects are things that happen immediately as a result of a tectonic hazard.
2 *Example* Tectonic hazard: Eyjafjallajökull eruption, 2010. The Iceland volcano Eyjafjallajökull erupted from March to May 2010. During April, the eruptions began to release enormous amounts of ash into the atmosphere. The aircraft industry was advised that flying through the volcanic ash could damage aircraft engines. As a result:
- 95 000 flights were cancelled, affecting around 10 million passengers
- losses to the aircraft industry have been estimated at £1.1 billion
- imports by air of fresh flowers from African countries such as Kenya to Europe were cancelled
- Kenya lost an estimated US$24 million from lost flower exports

- car manufacturers in Japan had to stop production because parts made in the EU could not be shipped to them in time.
3 *Example* First tectonic hazard: New Zealand earthquake, 2011; Second tectonic hazard: Haiti earthquake, 2010. On 22 February 2011, a 6.3 magnitude earthquake hit the city of Christchurch in New Zealand. New Zealand is a wealthy country with a GNI per capita of US$40020. The primary effects included:
- 185 people died, most because a multi-storey building collapsed due to the quake
- 3100 people were injured
- 100 000 buildings were damaged.
The Haiti earthquake happened on 12 January 2010. It was a magnitude 7 earthquake. Haiti is a very poor country, with a per capita GNI of just US$810. As in New Zealand, the epicentre of the quake was close to a major city, Port-au-Prince. Around 230 000 people were killed by the earthquake and 180000 buildings were destroyed. As in Christchurch, roads were destroyed; in Haiti, the main port was also destroyed.

5. Tectonic hazards: responses
1 (a) Maule Region, Chile
(b) There is no obvious relationship (correlation) between the magnitude of the earthquakes shown in Figure 1 and the number of deaths that occurred because of that earthquake. For example, both the Haiti earthquake and the earthquake in Papua, Indonesia, were magnitude 7.0, but the Haiti earthquake had perhaps 300 000 more deaths.
(c) Reason 1: If the earthquake happened in an area with very low numbers of people living there, that would help explain why the earthquake with the greatest magnitude did not have the highest number of deaths. Reason 2: *Example* If long-term responses to the earthquake were poorly funded and disorganised, diseases such as cholera and typhoid fever could have spread from people using water contaminated by human waste. These diseases can lead to high death tolls.
(d) *Example* After the 2011 earthquake and tsunami in Japan, a relatively wealthy country, the army cleared rubble off major roads in just two days, which meant emergency assistance could reach those in need, saving lives. The country had the systems and resources to organise a rapid immediate response to help people in urgent need. In Haiti, a very poor country, there were many problems in achieving an effective immediate response to the earthquake in 2010, due to the country's lack of resources and capacity. Around 98 per cent of roads were still not usable even a year later, which would have hindered rescue efforts and put lives at greater risk.

6. Living with tectonic hazards
1 Geothermal energy is providing heating for the house.
2 (a) It is clear to see that the population density is unevenly distributed. The area close to the location of the volcano is sparsely populated (0–10 people per km²), while the most densely populated area is on Java (over 1000 people per km²). No area on the map has the maximum population density shown in the key (5000+ people per km²).
(b) *Example* The volcano has provided ash, which enables fertile soil to develop. This means that people living closer to the volcano can grow more crops, for more food and greater income, even though they are at greater risk. *Other explanations: popular tourist destination (e.g. Bali); lack of awareness of threat; lack of economic means to move; family/emotional connection; highly paid jobs.*

7. Tectonic hazards: reducing risks
1 **C** The shaking of the ground (earthquakes)
2 Two from: tiltmeters, which show changes in the angle of the slope; COSPECS, which measure gas emissions; lasers or seismometers, which measure small earthquakes; satellite images, which detect the changing temperature of the surface; ultrasound, which measures whether magma is rising; thermometers, which measure temperature, which could indicate rising magma.
Example Method 1: Scientists can measure gases given off. If there is an increase in sulphur dioxide, this could indicate magma is rising to the surface. Method 2: Scientists could use satellite images, which use infrared to measure surface temperature around the volcano. If it is getting hotter, magma could be rising.
3 Satellite images use infrared which measures surface temperature. If there are elevated temperatures surrounding the volcano, this could indicate that magma is rising, causing the temperature of the surface to increase.

8. Global atmospheric circulation
1 **A** At **1**: Warm air rises at the Equator, creating low pressure; **C** At **2**: Cool air falls at around 30° north and south of the Equator
2 Apart from moving from belts of high pressure to low pressure, surface winds are also affected by the Earth's spin/Coriolis effect, which gives surface winds a curved path.
3 One way that heat is transferred is through the atmospheric circulation cells. The hot air rises and flows north and south of the Equator towards the poles. When it falls down towards the Earth's surface again at 30° north and south, some of the heat energy is transferred into the next circulation cell, which transfers it further north and south. *Another option is to describe heat transfer via surface winds or ocean currents. Surface winds are the winds we experience: blowing across the surface of the Earth to about a height of 10 metres. They are movements of air from high pressure to low pressure, and from warmer temperatures to cooler temperatures, so they also act to move warmer air to where temperatures are cooler. Ocean currents are movements of water within the ocean. Warm currents take warmer water towards the poles while cold currents take cold water from the poles towards the Equator.*

9. Tropical storms: distribution
1 The track of a tropical storm is the path that the storm takes, usually from its source to where it dissipates (loses enough energy to no longer be classified as a tropical storm).
2 *Example* The map shows the tropical storms being largely restricted to the tropics. There are three main reasons for this location. First, these storms are powered by warm ocean temperatures – the seawater needs to be above 26.5°C and these temperatures are only found in late summer and autumn in the tropics. Second is the effect of latitude. Tropical storms mostly occur between 5° and 20° north and south of the Equator. They do not occur closer to the Equator because the Coriolis effect from the Equator to 5° north and south of the Equator is too weak to give the spin to wind movements that help to form the rotating air movements of tropical storms. Third is the zone of low pressure around the Equator, which generates thunderstorms. Tropical storms often form as several thunderstorms join together. No one is completely sure what makes a tropical storm form, but the distribution suggests these factors are important. It is certainly true that tropical storms form over warm tropical seas and move inland.

143

10. Tropical storms: causes and structure

1 (a) 3 = The air spirals up rapidly which causes high winds.
4 = The air condenses as it rises and cools, forming huge clouds and heavy rain.
5 = In the centre of the storm, air falls, forming the eye.
(b) Factor 1: High humidity is important because <u>there needs to be a lot of moisture in the atmosphere to condense out and power the storm.</u> Factor 2: Pre-existing low pressure disturbances are important because <u>tropical storms usually form when smaller storms come together.</u>

11. Tropical storms: changes

1 **C** The Saffir-Simpson scale
2 Wind speed is one of the main ways in which tropical storms are measured and compared with each other. Typhoon Haiyan's highest wind speed was 130 km/h faster than Hurricane Sandy. This means that <u>Typhoon Haiyan was a higher magnitude storm than Hurricane Sandy, in a category called a 'super typhoon'. A second measure of magnitude could be the amount of damage caused by the storms. Both Typhoon Haiyan and Hurricane Sandy caused large numbers of fatalities, but Typhoon Haiyan caused over 6000 more than Hurricane Sandy. This suggests that Typhoon Haiyan was a category 5 storm, causing catastrophic damage, while Hurricane Sandy, while still very destructive, was at a lower level of magnitude – perhaps category 3.</u>
3 Climate change leading to global warming affects ocean temperatures because the oceans are the Earth's major area for heat storage. A warmer atmosphere means warmer oceans. This could affect the intensity of tropical storms because tropical storms become more powerful as ocean temperatures increase above 26.5°C. It is also possible that tropical storms could start to occur in areas where ocean temperatures have previously been too cool. If those areas start to have ocean temperatures of 26.5°C and higher, then the distribution of tropical storms could increase.

12. Tropical storms: effects

1 Tropical storms can bring extreme weather conditions such as strong winds, <u>heavy rain and storm surges. The primary effects of a tropical storm are the immediate impacts of the storm itself: the deaths and destruction to property caused by the extreme weather conditions.</u>
2 Low-lying coastlines are vulnerable to storm surge flooding, caused by low air pressure within tropical storms.
3 *Example* Typhoon Haiyan: a category 5 tropical storm in the Philippines in November 2013. Around 600 000 people had to leave their homes, especially in Tacloban where 90 per cent of the city was destroyed. Around 400 000 people were housed in 1100 emergency camps. Nearly 10 000 schools were destroyed, which meant children missed out on education. Farmers were not able to grow rice on the salt-contaminated soil and rice prices rose by 12 per cent. There were outbreaks of disease because of sewage contamination and because hospitals had been destroyed.
One reason for such severe secondary effects was that Typhoon Haiyan was the strongest tropical storm to have made landfall in the Philippines that has ever been measured, so emergency measures that would have protected people from a normal tropical storm failed: for example, evacuation shelters were destroyed by the flying debris or were not high enough to escape the 5-metre storm surge. A second reason was that the devastation caused by Typhoon Haiyan blocked roads, ports and airports, making it difficult for rescue and relief operations to get to the worst-hit areas and start to help people. This was also affected by the heavy rain that followed the tropical storm. A third reason was that the Philippines is an LIC. Many of the houses in the areas hit by Typhoon Haiyan were made of wood and not very strong, which meant large-scale destruction of property and high numbers of people being made homeless.

13. Tropical storms: responses

1 (a) *Example* Apart from rescuing people left in danger by the primary or secondary effects of a tropical storm, one other immediate response to a tropical storm is <u>ensuring people have clean water to drink.</u> *Other options: preventing looting of homes; ensuring people are warm enough and have shelter; moving dead bodies of people and animals to reduce risk of disease and to reduce distress; the government can make emergency funds available immediately to help with rescues and evacuations; organising the armed forces to help with providing immediate help for survivors.*
(b) The flooded streets would make it very difficult for road vehicles to reach this location, so <u>rescue attempts would need to be made by air or boat. This can be challenging because only a few people can be rescued at a time, which can lead to people panicking or getting angry.</u>
2 Two from: improving monitoring of tropical storms so there is more time for people to evacuate; improving the evacuation process so that more people feel able to leave their homes; improving public education so people know what to do when a tropical storm is forecast; improving communication of warnings about tropical storms and evacuation requirements (for example, using social media); increasing flood defences or installing new defences; improving the community's resilience (for example, by rebuilding damaged homes with flood protection measures, such as building them on stilts).

14. Tropical storms: reducing risks

1 (a) **C** Precipitation data – likely rainfall levels
(b) *Example* First way: Scientists can analyse the data produced by monitoring the tropical storm and find out useful information, such as what local factors intensify tropical storms. This can help planning and protection measures. Second way: <u>Monitoring data is used to forecast (predict) what the storm will do, especially after landfall. This is vital for reducing risk as it informs evacuation plans and the deployment of protection measures.</u> *Other options: Monitoring means that people can be warned about tropical storms, allowing them to take measures to reduce damage to their property (for example, securing garden furniture that might get blown around in the storm, fixing shutters to windows or boarding up windows to prevent them being blown in); monitoring means people can prepare for the storm (for example, filling containers with water in case of problems with water supply, getting torches and battery-operated radios ready in case of power problems, possibly moving valuable items to higher, safer places in the house in case of flooding, getting ready to evacuate (by packing food, water, clothing, key documents, and so on).*

15. UK: weather hazards

1 (a) 36.2%
(b) One from: heatstroke; people with pre-existing health conditions may suffer; stationary cars can quickly become very hot inside, which could put pets and children at risk.
(c) One from: hypothermia (when core body temperature drops below 35°C); health conditions that are worsened when the body is under extreme stress; risk of accidents on ice; property can be damaged (e.g. burst water pipes caused by ice inside the pipe expanding).
(d) *Example* Hazard 1: River flooding – both long duration and high intensity rainfall can result in rivers exceeding their carrying capacity and flooding populated areas along their banks. Hazard 2: <u>Flash flooding, especially when the rainfall is very intense or where the</u> <u>soil's infiltration capacity is exceeded and large volumes of surface runoff are produced.</u> *Other options could include: dangerous driving conditions caused by large amounts of surface water on the roads; so much water entering urban drainage systems that sewage is washed into rivers instead of travelling to sewage treatment works; landslides caused when slopes become destabilised due to over-saturation of the soil.*

16. UK: extreme weather

1 Your answer will depend on the example that you have studied. In the Paper 1 exam, questions like this will be marked according to a mark scheme. The best answers will meet requirements for three assessment objectives (AOs): AO1, AO2 and AO3.
• **AO1** is about showing your knowledge of locations, places, processes, environments and different scales. For this answer, AO1 will relate to your knowledge of the different ways in which your extreme weather event impacted on people and property.
• **AO2** is about showing your geographical understanding of concepts about and interrelationships between places, environments and processes. For this answer, AO2 will relate to the way you understand the concepts involved in the question: what are economic impacts, what are social impacts, what are environmental impacts, for example.
• **AO3** is about applying your knowledge and understanding to interpret, analyse and evaluate geographical information and issues and to make judgements. In this question, you are asked to make a judgement about the extent to which economic impacts are more significant than social or environmental impacts.

17. UK: more extreme weather

1 (a) **B** Everywhere in the UK experienced mean average temperatures that were above the long-term average for 1961–1990; **C** The parts of England that experienced the highest above-average mean maximum temperatures also included an area that experienced 75–85 per cent less rainfall than the long-term average for 1961–1990.
(b) *Example* Extreme weather can be defined as weather that is significantly different from average weather conditions. The temperature map (Figure 1) provides good evidence of 2015 being extreme because nowhere in the UK recorded average temperatures that were the same as or below the long-term average for 1961–1990. Some parts of the UK were 1.5°C warmer on average than <u>the long-term average, which is a significantly higher figure. The map for rainfall (Figure 2) also provides some evidence of weather becoming more extreme – significantly different from the average – because it shows that in 2015, large areas of central, southern and south-east England had between 5 and 10 per cent less rainfall than the long-term average, with small areas in the east of England and Scotland experiencing significantly less: 15–25 per cent below the long-term average.</u> *Other options: You could also point to areas of significantly above long-term average rainfall amounts as evidence of increasing rainfall, supporting your answer with evidence from the map.*

18. Climate change: evidence

1 (a) **D** Antarctica
(b) Figure 1 shows that atmospheric concentrations of CO_2 changed significantly from the end of the last Ice Age until 9000 years ago. At the end of the last Ice Age, 21 000 years ago, CO_2 levels were below <u>190 ppmv (parts per million by volume). Around 18 000 years ago the levels began to increase, until about 10 000 years ago they had reached a level of between 260 and 270 ppmv. This provides evidence of past climate change because increased levels of atmospheric CO_2 are associated with warmer temperatures, while lower levels of CO_2 are associated with colder temperatures, such as</u>

those of an Ice Age. The evidence for these changing levels of atmospheric CO_2 comes from ice cores, which provide a reliable record of how much CO_2 is in the atmosphere. The evidence is recorded as follows: as snow falls, air is trapped between the flakes as they settle. As the snow is compressed under more snow into ice, the air is preserved as bubbles within the ice. This also preserves the different gases in the air and it is possible to work out from the proportion of the different gases what the concentrations of greenhouse gases like CO_2 and methane (CH_4) were for the different layers in the ice. An ice core is a vertical sample through all the different layers of ice, which can be counted back like tree rings, so it is possible to work out what the concentrations of different atmospheric gases were at different times for as far back as the ice sheet was in existence (up to 800 000 years in the case of some Antarctic ice domes).

19. Climate change: possible causes

1 (a) *Example* Reason 1: The amount of heat the Earth receives from the Sun varies because of changes to the orbital cycle, which could trigger ice ages; Reason 2: *Options include: changes in solar output (less solar energy = cooler global temperatures); increased volcanic activity (ash clouds block some incoming solar energy, leading to cooler global temperatures).*
   (b) Agriculture, because it involves removing natural vegetation like forest, which is a natural store of carbon, and because agricultural machinery has high carbon emissions; deforestation, because this removes the natural carbon store provided by trees, which also soak up carbon dioxide.
2 100 ppm (parts per million)

20. Climate change: effects

1 One from: melting ice caps; melting glaciers; rising sea levels.
2 First way: If temperatures increase, some areas of the world could have an increase in food production because the growing season will be longer and crops can be grown in higher latitudes, such as in Russia; Second way: Other areas of the world could have a decrease in food production because drier conditions will inhibit crop growth, such as wheat production in the USA or Canada, which will impact on their exports.
3 *Example* In the summer, drought and water shortages could become more common, especially in the south. Farmers may have to change their crops, and crop yields could decrease through changing rainfall patterns. Some plants and animals may struggle to survive with their existing patterns of distribution. Fish and marine ecosystems may also be affected by rising water temperatures, causing loss of habitat and migration. Increased rainfall amounts, and increased rainfall intensity, could increase flooding from surface runoff and also river flooding, as higher sea levels would increase flooding from the sea and increase rates of coastal erosion.

21. Mitigating climate change

1 (a) One from: speed – it would be much quicker to plant wide areas by aerial reforestation than by hand; cost – although the capsules and the plane would cost money, this is likely to be much less than the cost of transport, wages, food and support for a team planting trees by hand; a more natural forest environment – trees would land randomly, like wind-borne seeds, rather than being planted in rows.
   (b) Mitigation means reducing the severity or impact of something.
   (c) Carbon dioxide (CO_2) is a greenhouse gas, and the increasing CO_2 levels in the atmosphere linked to human activity are a major cause of climate change. Trees and other vegetation pull CO_2 from the air through photosynthesis and they store this carbon in roots, trunks, stems and leaves. Replanting areas with trees

is a good way to reduce the causes of climate change, although it is important that the trees are allowed to mature since older trees are better at storing carbon and cutting down trees releases carbon back into the atmosphere. The best way of using tree-planting for climate change mitigation would be to combine it with strategies to reduce deforestation.

22. Adapting to climate change

1 (a) One from: farmers need to water crops more in warmer conditions; people to water plants and grass, which need more water in warmer conditions; people take more showers in hot weather; people and animals need to drink more in warmer weather.
   (b) *Example* The amount of water a toilet uses when it flushes can be reduced by fitting smaller flushes or adding objects to cisterns to reduce the amount of water used in each flush. *Other options: people can take shorter showers or fit showers with water-reducing shower heads; washing machines and dishwaters can be used less frequently or used with eco-settings that use less water; people can collect water in water butts from winter rainfall to water their gardens with, or recycle bath water and shower water for watering gardens; people can wash their cars less or avoid using pressure hoses that waste a lot of water; water meters can be fitted to houses so people are charged for the amount of water they use, which tends to reduce water use over time.*
2 (a) If climate change means rainfall events become more intense, this can lead to the infiltration capacity of the soil being rapidly exceeded. This results in increased surface runoff and flash flooding. Climate change also leads to longer rainfall duration. Continuous rain over several days means the ground becomes saturated and further rainfall cannot infiltrate, leading to increased surface runoff.
   (b) While the impact of rainfall on bare soil compacts the soil and increases surface runoff, plant cover intercepts rainfall, reducing compaction, increasing infiltration and absorbing water through roots.
   (c) **B** Increasing groundwater availability; **C** Reducing the risk of surface water flooding

23. A small-scale UK ecosystem

1 A community of living organisms (plants and animals) and their physical environment (sunlight, air, water, rock and soil) which are all linked together and often depend on each other.
2 (a) A producer: one from rushes, water lily, green algae, some of the bacteria; A consumer: one from frog, small fish, large fish, some bacteria, heron; A decomposer: bacteria
   (b) A producer can convert energy from the Sun into energy stored in plant tissue through the process of photosynthesis. A consumer cannot convert energy from the Sun in this way, but relies on eating producers or other consumers in order to obtain the energy needed for life.

24. Ecosystems and change

1 (a) **D** Reduced surface runoff
   (b) The biomass store is the largest store in the rainforest ecosystem, which means that most nutrients are actually in biomass rather than in the litter layer or soil. The removal of rainforest biomass would remove these nutrients from the ecosystem. Heavy precipitation would continue, as would rapid leaching of nutrients from the soil. As a result, soil fertility would decrease rapidly as the nutrients left in the soil store were leached out.

25. Global ecosystems

1 **D** Desert ecosystem
2 Tropical rainforests are found in South and Central America, Africa and parts of SE Asia. Their distribution is closely tied to within a few degrees north and south of the Equator.
3 Characteristics include: long, cold winters – seven months of the year have average temperatures below zero degrees; low precipitation – below

500 mm for the whole year; very cold winters – three months with temperatures below minus 20 degrees; short, cool summers – maximum summer temperatures around 12°C.

26. Rainforest characteristics

1 **D** Herb layer or forest floor
2 Plants compete for sunlight.
3 Your completed diagram labelling should be something like the this:
   Litter layer   Shallow roots
   Heavy rainfall flows down through soil
   leaching out nutrients
   Weathering adds nutrients (minerals)

27. Interdependences and adaptations

1 **C** The soil
2 *Example* Feature 1: In the centre of the picture there are buttress roots of a tree. Feature 2: The forest has several layers at different heights. *Other option: The leaves have drip tips.*
3 *Example* Monkeys have evolved gripping hands and feet so they can balance high up in the canopy to forage for fruit, nuts and berries. *Other options: some animals have long tails to help them balance as they climb – some tails are prehensile (can grip) as well; animals on the dark forest floor have evolved excellent night vision; some birds have highly colourful plumage so potential mates can see them through the dense rainforest vegetation; some birds have short, powerful wings that enable them to manoeuvre through the canopy; some animals have camouflage to hide them from predators among the leaves of the canopy – some even look like leaves.*

28. Deforestation: causes

1 (a) In 1975, the area shown was almost entirely covered in forest. By 1992, one main road running east to west is running through the forest, with smaller roads extending off it north and south into the forest. By 2001 large areas (almost 75 per cent) of the forest have been removed in the area around the roads.
   (b) Two from the following:
   • **Commercial farming and ranching** Large-scale farming needs the land to be cleared of almost all trees; it cannot be conducted as economically when crops or livestock are mixed in with tropical rainforest vegetation. There is a high demand for more food crops, for meat from livestock and more biofuels around the world, and this demand makes it very profitable to clear rainforest for farming. Commercial farming often follows logging.
   • **Subsistence farming** Although traditional methods of subsistence farming are sustainable and may even have become part of tropical rainforest ecosystems, population growth means that traditional slash-and-burn agriculture no longer has long periods where the land is left fallow to recover its vegetation. Instead, there is so much pressure for land that each plot is used repeatedly for crops until it is stripped of nutrients, at which point the farming family needs to clear another plot of land, increasing deforestation.
   • **Logging** While loggers are usually only interested in particular types of trees, it is much cheaper to clear the whole area of all trees and sell the land to commercial farmers than to select only a few trees for felling and extract those from the rainforest (selective logging). Logging is big business because many tropical trees produce excellent timber which can be sold for high prices.
   • **Mining** Mining is associated with tropical rainforest deforestation, particularly in the case of open-cast mining. Usually the cheapest way to get to buried minerals is to dig a massive pit rather than to dig mine shafts and mine the minerals from underground. Mining also needs transport out of the area – roads and railways, which also require forest to be cleared.

29. Deforestation: impacts

1 Tropical rainforest biomass acts as a carbon sink – an enormous store of carbon. Because of this, when rainforest trees are cut down and burnt to clear the land, that store of carbon is released back into the atmosphere.

2 *Example* The biggest nutrient store in the tropical rainforest ecosystem is biomass. There is relatively little in the soil, so once biomass is removed through deforestation, there is little organic matter in the soil to hold it together and prevent the soil being eroded. *Other option: Tree cover provides protection for the soil from the heavy rainfall of the tropical rainforest ecosystem through interception. When that cover is gone because of deforestation, rainfall falls directly onto the soil and soil erosion can become very rapid.*

3 Your answer will depend on your case study. In many ways, rainforest deforestation tends to have positive impacts on a country's economic development, which is why it happens. The agricultural area of the country increases, which benefits the poorest people who otherwise would be landless – instead they can feed themselves and some will become prosperous farmers and make money for the country. Deforestation for commercial agriculture can be important for developing export markets in crops and livestock; for example, soybeans in Brazil or beef from cattle raising. Logging has been important for economic development because many tropical hardwoods are extremely valuable timber with special properties; for example, very strong wood, wood that takes a deep polish and/or wood that is resistant to rotting. Deforestation to make way for dams and HEP schemes helps economic development because it provides secure supplies of fresh water to cities, regulates rivers from flooding (making farming less vulnerable to floods) and provides cheap electric power for industry and housing. However, the negative impacts of deforestation can also potentially harm economic development; for example, the loss of fertile farmland through soil erosion or the loss of rainforest which could have attracted tourism.

30. Rainforest value

1 *Example* Trees and plants absorb carbon dioxide from the atmosphere. They therefore reduce CO_2 levels in the atmosphere (about 20 per cent of the CO_2 produced by human activity is absorbed by the rainforests) and reduce global warming. *Other options: Trees and plants also give off oxygen as part of photosynthesis. They are major contributors to global oxygen levels: about 20 per cent of the world's oxygen comes from the rainforests. Rainforests also exchange huge amounts of water with the atmosphere: they soak it up from the soil and trap it on their leaves and stems, releasing it back via transpiration and evaporation. This has significant impacts on local and regional climates.*

2 Your answer could include:
• timber goods for use in building, making furniture, ornaments, and so on
• source of medicines – some important modern medicines have their origins in tropical rainforest plants and animal products; many more medicines could be found from tropical rainforest organisms
• source of food for local people and for export – for example, food from rainforest plants, nuts and berries (– cocoa, for example, which is used to make chocolate) was originally a rainforest plant
• ecotourism – the rainforest is a popular tourist destination, usually with tourists who want to contribute to rainforest conservation and to minimise their impact on the rainforest ecosystem
• carbon sequestration – rainforest plants store CO_2 in their tissues, keeping it out of the atmosphere
• preventing soil erosion – rainforest vegetation intercepts the heavy, frequent rainfall while rainforest litter adds nutrients to the soil and rainforest vegetation roots help bind the rainforest soil together
• absorption of CO_2 – rainforest plants absorb CO_2 from the atmosphere
• capture, store and slow release of water – rainforest plants take up water through their roots and store it in their tissues, then release it slowly through the process of transpiration; rainforests act like giant sponges, slowly releasing water through the year and affecting the distribution of precipitation in surrounding areas
• biodiversity – rainforests support the most biodiverse land-based ecosystem on Earth
• home for indigenous peoples – tribes of people for whom the rainforest is home.

31. Sustainable management

1 (a) The rate of deforestation has declined almost every year between 2004 and 2011, although it did increase very slightly from 2007 to 2008.
(b) Three from the following:
• International agreements have been made to reduce rainforest deforestation, leading to national commitments (like Brazil's commitment to reduce deforestation to 1900 square miles a year by 2017).
• There has been conservation and protection of areas of the rainforest through national parks or other nature reserves.
• Deforested areas, such as on farmland and areas of cattle ranches, have been replanted.
• Debt-for-conservation swaps have been made, in which poorer countries promise to protect areas of the forest in return for a reduction in international debts.
• Alternative sources of income from the forest have been created, such as ecotourism or sustainable timber production, rather than illegal logging.
• Selective logging has been practised, rather than wholesale logging.

32. Hot deserts: characteristics

1 (a) **A** < 250 mm
(b) One from the following:
• Most deserts are located between 20° and 30° north and south of the Equator. Warm air rising from the Equator travels north and south of the Equator and then cools and descends. As it descends, it creates high pressure belts that are characterised by largely cloudless skies.
• Some hot deserts are located in the rain shadows of mountain ranges; for example, in the south west of the USA.
• The location of some desert regions is influenced by continentality: moisture from oceans has all been precipitated by the time it reaches the continental interior. Temperatures are also influenced by land heating up and cooling down more rapidly than the oceans.
• Some deserts are located on coasts where cold ocean currents cool the air passing over it, which then warms and rises over the land creating a rain shadow.
(c) *Example* The high pressure atmospheric conditions in hot deserts mean that they usually have clear skies during the day and night, so there is no cloud layer to trap heat radiating from the ground. During the day the desert surface becomes very hot, producing very high daytime temperatures. At night this heat radiates straight back into the atmosphere because there is no cloud layer to trap it. *Other option: Deserts have a high albedo: without vegetation or water to absorb heat, the desert surface reflects heat. This means it cools very rapidly once the source of heat (the Sun) disappears.*

33. The hot desert ecosystem

1 (a) *Example* First plant adaptation: Some plants, like the globemallow, have very deep root systems. These roots can reach down to groundwater a long way beneath the surface. Second plant adaptation: Some plants have spines instead of leaves, which reduces the amount of water loss from transpiration. *Other options: ability to store water; wide, shallow roots to maximise absorption of any rainwater that does fall; tough seedcases that can tolerate long periods of drought and even fire; spines to deter animals that might try to eat them.*
(b) Two from: being nocturnal; living in burrows during the day; sleeping in shaded areas; hibernating through long periods of drought; ability to survive with very little water (e.g. absorbing the water needed from food or through the skin from fog or dew); ability to store water in body tissues.

34. Development opportunities

1 (a) *Example* A different culture – Middle Eastern cuisine, history and architecture. *Other options: climate – hot and dry; a sense of adventure in an extreme environment; desert animals and wildlife – such as camels, desert flowers; for people who live in places with cold winters, spending winter where it is warm but not too hot.*
(b) Your answer will depend on your case study. *Options include mineral extraction, farming, energy and tourism. Example* Solar power is a development opportunity in the Mojave Desert, south-west USA. For example, the Ivanpah Solar Power Facility, located on the Nevada-California border, has a 370 MW power generating capacity, the largest in the world for solar power.
(c) Your answer will depend on your case study. *Here you are not being asked to evaluate this statement, but* support *it. You need to select information from your case study to show that extracting fossil fuels from the desert and/or generating solar power is a growth area.*

35. Development challenges

1 (a) **C** 56 million cubic metres per day
(b) Disadvantage: Desalination is expensive. It requires a large amount of energy to power the desalination process. Solar power can generate some of this energy in hot desert environments, but not all. Advantage: Desalination can provide fresh water, which is essential for development in hot desert regions, when that region is near a coast or a supply of brackish water (e.g. a salt lake or inland sea).

36. Desertification: causes

1 (a) **A** The persistent degradation of dryland ecosystems to create desert-like conditions
(b) Two from the following:
• In semi-arid regions, climate change appears to be making droughts more common and longer-lasting, and making rain less reliable. This puts pressure on vegetation and, in combination with other factors, makes soil erosion more likely.
• Population growth increases the pressure on semi-arid areas because more people want land, which pushes the least fortunate onto marginal land already prone to soil degradation. *Other points: More people also means land is farmed more, with less time to recover soil nutrients. It also means more livestock is pastured on vulnerable land, and more demand for fuelwood, leading to faster deforestation.*
• Trees and bushes help stabilise the soil and their roots draw up water into the soil, raising the water table. *Other points: Their leaves intercept intense rainfall and reduce soil compaction, reducing surface runoff and increasing infiltration into the soil. Removing trees for fuel increases soil erosion and makes desertification more likely.*
• Overgrazing means the grasses and plants that stabilise dryland soils are eaten and topsoil is broken up by trampling, making it more easily eroded by the wind. This makes soil erosion more likely.
• Over-cultivation breaks down the structure of the soil by ploughing. Removing nutrients from the soil makes it more crumbly and more vulnerable to wind erosion. *Other points: Leaving fields bare after harvest increases soil erosion. Raising repeated crops from the land without time for the soil to recover dries it out and changes the*

structure of the soil so it erodes more easily. Over-irrigation can also cause salinisation, in which mineral salts are deposited in the topsoil, making it too salty for anything to grow.

37. Desertification: reducing the risk

1 (a) Way 1: One reason for desertification is that over-cultivation of the soil means it loses its organic matter and nutrients, dries up and becomes easily eroded by wind and water. The Fallow Band System helps to keep organic matter and nutrients in the soil because the bands are not used for crops, so they recover nutrients, and the organic matter that grows on them is ploughed back into the soil. Way 2: Another reason for desertification is wind erosion. The Fallow Band System reduces wind erosion because the bands of fallow land are set at right angles to the prevailing wind (or at right angles to the direction the strongest storms usually come from). Soil eroded by the wind from farmed parts of the fields will be deposited in the fallow bands, because the wind speed will drop among the weeds growing on them. This soil is then trapped on the fallow bands and will contribute to improved yields when the bands are ploughed up and sown for crops in the next season.

(b) One from: it does not need specialised technology or machinery to set up or maintain – farmers just have to not plough or dig up bands of land; it is free – farmers will lose some income because they will not be able to use all their field for crops, but they should get better crops, so it should pay for itself; it does not require specialist knowledge to understand; it should start to show benefits for local people within two years, so people can decide quickly about the benefits and costs; it works with the environment, using natural systems rather than relying on chemical fertilisers, herbicides and pesticides.

38. Cold environments: characteristics

1 (a) Cold environments are environments that experience freezing temperatures (below zero/0°C) for long periods of the year.

(b) A Seven months

(c) *Example* Characteristic 1: The main vegetation is low-lying grasses and mosses. Characteristic 2: It is usually treeless. *Other options: low biodiversity; poor drainage (bogs and ponds); short growing season of 50–60 days (plants flower rapidly in spring); most nutrients in the litter layer; large insect populations in the short summer.*

(d) One from:
• treeless because the conditions are too dry for trees (sometimes less than 250 mm per year: cold desert)
• low biodiversity because the freezing temperatures halt the nutrient cycle and make this a low-nutrient environment
• poor drainage because of the permafrost – a layer of permanently frozen ground – which is impermeable
• short but intense growing season – although there are only 50–60 days for plants to grow in, the days are very long so plants get a lot of light
• nutrients in the litter layer because decomposition stops during the long winters
• large insect populations – and population booms and crashes – because the waterlogged conditions and warm summer temperatures are perfect for insects.

39. The cold environment ecosystem

1 (a) First adaptation: The bearberry has small leaves to minimise water loss in this dry environment; Second adaptation, one from: growing close to the ground minimises damage from the strong tundra winds; growing close to the ground reduces damage from wind-blown ice crystals; its small dark green leaves can photosynthesise in very low temperatures; it can produce flowers very rapidly as soon as spring temperatures begin to rise.

(b) *See page 156 for answer.*

40. Development opportunities

1 Your answer will depend on your case study. The best answers for this sort of question will have paid careful attention to the question wording. In this case, **assess the opportunities** means you need to consider the extent to which different kinds of development are options for the cold environment that you have studied. So, for example, if you have studied the Antarctic as your cold environment, you would need to consider mineral extraction as a development opportunity but then conclude that, for the present at least, mineral extraction is not an opportunity for Antarctica because of it being prohibited by the 1959 Antarctic Treaty. However, for tourism you might conclude that, although tourist numbers are controlled, as are the places in Antarctica that they can visit and the way they need to behave, there is still significant opportunity for tourism to develop further because there is demand from people wanting to visit and potential tourists are prepared to pay a lot for their chance to visit Antarctica.

Make sure your answer uses relevant and accurate detail from your case study location (Assessment Objective 1).

41. Development challenges

1 (a) **A** Extreme low temperature;
B Inaccessibility

(b) The pipeline needs to be raised above the ground in areas affected by permafrost because if it were buried, the pipeline would buckle as the earth around it moved when the top layers of the permafrost melted in spring and then froze again in winter.

(c) Your answers will depend on your case study. *Options include: extreme temperature, inaccessibility, provision of buildings and infrastructure.*

42. Fragile wilderness

1 (a) Acid precipitation damages plants, kills insect larvae in ponds and lakes and kills the soil bacteria responsible for decomposition. Cold environments are vulnerable to this sort of damage because migratory birds and mammals depend on insects in the summer.

(b) *Example* Climate change is the biggest threat to cold environments because warming temperatures completely alter the processes that are fundamental to cold environments. In the Arctic, the average air temperature has increased about 5°C over the last 100 years: warming is happening twice as fast in the Arctic as elsewhere in the world because as it loses more and more highly-reflective snow, the land and sea underneath absorb more energy from the Sun, making it warmer. As a result, the extent of sea ice has decreased by between 12 and 30 per cent over the last 40 years and, if global warming continues, in another 40 years there will probably be no summer sea ice at all.

This warming is a major threat to the Arctic because Arctic life is adapted to a cold environment and the change is so rapid that many life forms will not be able to adapt quickly enough to the new conditions.

Another threat is the increasing acidification of Arctic seawater due to the increased amount of carbon dioxide it has absorbed. Cold oceans are acidifying twice as fast as warmer oceans and this has enormous impacts on sea life. As a consequence, some fish species could be badly affected, which would have impacts on the fishing industry.

Warming temperatures are also a threat because the Arctic is now becoming a much easier place for humans to live, work and travel. This means the Arctic is increasingly accessible for development opportunities, which is good for the countries involved, but is a major threat to the natural habitats of this cold environment – for example, from oil spills and other forms of pollution, which are highly damaging to cold environments, as well as from increased numbers of wildfires and acid precipitation from industrial developments.

43. Managing cold environments

1 (a) 30 398 (30 397.6 rounded up to the nearest whole number)

(b) Visitor numbers are carefully controlled (no more than 400 people a day, with no visitors from 10 pm to 2 am) for three main reasons. It reduces soil erosion along footpaths (Antarctica is conserved as a natural wilderness and all human impacts are minimised); it reduces the chance of vegetation trampling (cold environments are low-nutrient environments, which means that plants grow slowly and damage takes a long time to be repaired); and it reduces the chance that wildlife will be frightened by the visitors. For example, if visitors frighten seabirds while they are nesting, parent birds could fly away and abandon their eggs or chicks. The location could stop being a breeding ground for birds. This would be a major environmental impact that needs to be avoided if at all possible. Also, the visitors come to see the wildlife so, if tourism is to be sustainable, it needs to be controlled. Ship numbers are controlled to reduce the numbers of tourists and the disturbance to wildlife, and to reduce the risk of oil spills or other environmental pollution.

44. Physical landscapes in the UK

1 (a) A = River Thames; B = River Severn;
C = River Tyne

(b) River Trent

(c) D = Pennines, E = Dartmoor

45. Types of wave

1 Destructive: **2** Occur in stormy conditions and **3** Responsible for erosion; Constructive: **1** Low wave energy and
4 Help transport material

2 Movement of water up the beach

3 Waves hitting the south-west coast of England will have large amounts of energy because the waves have travelled a long distance. These powerful waves are destructive, with their backwash being greater than their swash.

4 The energy of a wave depends on three main factors: the fetch, the speed of the wind and the length of time the wind has been blowing. *Example* On the SW coast of England, the fetch is bigger because the prevailing wind travels the width of the Atlantic Ocean. This will mean that there is no land in the way to divert wave energy, so waves become more powerful. In stormy conditions, wind speeds increase and this makes the surface waves taller, making them more powerful. *Other option: write the answer from the viewpoint of less powerful waves.*

46. Weathering and mass movement

1 (a) Mass movement

(b) *Example* Factor 1: The wet weather will have saturated the rocks with water, so the rock is heavier and looser, making landslides more common. Factor 2: Longshore drift has been stopped by the building of groynes further up the coast, which has removed the natural protection provided by a sandy beach. *Other options: soft sandstone rock, which may have become softer and more weathered by the heavy rain; undercutting of the cliff by wave action, which would have contributed by making the slope less stable; people walking on top of the cliff.*

2 freezes, scree

47. Erosion, transport, deposition

1 (a) **D** When the force of destructive waves pounding the base of cliffs compresses air into cracks in the rocks

(b) First factor: More powerful waves due to stronger winds. Second factor could include: a longer fetch (which makes waves more powerful); the depth of the sea floor as the wave approaches the coast (waves lose power from friction with the sea bed); if the climate means there are lots of nights where temperatures dip below freezing but days where the temperatures rise above freezing again; rocks with lots of cracks or joints in them; weak rocks that are eroded quickly; human activities that increase the power of waves (e.g. big ships creating large wakes).

2   *See page 156 for answer.*

48. Erosion landforms

1   (a) U = Stump, V = Stack, W = Arch,
X = Wave-cut platform,
Y = Wave-cut notch, Z = Cliff
(b) *See page 156 for answer.*

49. Deposition landforms

1   (a) A spit
(b) *See page 156 for answer.*

50. Coastal landforms

1   A: bar; B: lagoon

2   Softer rock, such as clays and sands, will provide less resistance than harder rock, therefore increasing the impact of the wave energy. At Swanage Bay, for example, the soft rock means that the cliffs are retreating and forming bays, containing beaches. Harder rocks, such as Portland Stone or the Purbeck Beds, are more resistant to erosion and therefore they remain jutting out into the sea, creating headlands, such as Durlston Head. It is likely that the headlands feature landforms such as caves, arches, stacks and stumps, together with wave-cut platforms where the headland has been fully removed. Further along the coast, deposition, over many thousands of years, might have formed landforms such as spits or tombolas, depending on the strength and direction of longshore drift.
The southern coastline of Dorset is a concordant coast, where the bands of hard and soft rock are parallel to the coastline. Here, headlands and bays are not common. Instead, there are coves where the sea has broken through weak points in the band of hard limestone and eroded into the softer rock behind it.

51. Hard engineering

1   (a) Rock armour (rip-rap)
(b) Rock armour works by absorbing and deflecting the energy of waves before they reach the defended structure. The size and mass of the rip-rap material absorbs the impact energy of waves, while the gaps between the rocks trap and slow the flow of water, lessening its ability to erode soil or structures on the coast.

2   Groynes are used to stop the process of longshore drift. The sediment gets trapped and helps build up the beach, which acts as a natural defence against wave energy because it breaks waves early, therefore reducing their erosive power and protecting the land behind.

3   Hard defences are normally only used where the benefits of providing expensive defences are significantly higher than the costs of building and maintaining the defences: to protect important infrastructure, houses, and so on. Examples include the Bacton gas terminal in North Norfolk, where the rest of the coast has 'retreat' or 'do nothing' management.

52. Soft engineering and managed retreat

1   (a) D Coastal realignment
(b) *Example* Advantage: Beach nourishment widens beaches so they provide more protection to the coast. Disadvantage: The process has to be repeated after each winter, or every couple of winters. *Other options: beaches have to be closed while nourishment takes place; marine plants and animals are at risk during beach nourishment because the process dumps sand and pebbles onto existing habitats; the process is expensive (because of the need to constantly repeat it); erosion of re-nourished beaches is often faster than natural beaches.*
(c) Dune regeneration usually involves creating new dunes or stabilising older dunes that have

become eroded. Dunes are effective at reducing coastal erosion because they form a natural barrier that slows down wind speeds, leading to deposition of wind-eroded material, and also slows down water erosion. Dunes gradually stabilise sandy beaches helping to prevent coastal erosion because vegetation holds soil together, as does organic matter in the soil, so that it is not easily eroded by wind and water.

2   Reason 1: Soft engineering techniques help to prevent erosion by mimicking natural processes, such as dune regeneration and beach nourishment, and as a result can minimise environmental impacts on the area.
Reason 2: Hard engineering techniques do not mimic natural processes, are often visually polluting and can have negative environmental impacts further down the coast.

53. Coastal management

1   *Example* A sea wall – this would prevent further erosion of the coast to 'hold the line'. *Other options: rock armour (for the exposed coastline areas); groynes for the more sheltered bay areas (where erosion from longshore drift might also be a problem).*

2   Your answer might include the following.
Costs:
•   no financial cost of building defences if the coast is stable
•   loss of farmland
•   people losing their homes and businesses
•   loss of roads and pathways
•   social and political problems associated with people feeling they have been abandoned when they should be protected from this type of threat
•   environmental problems to do with loss of natural habitat.
Benefits:
•   the money can be used elsewhere if the coast is stable
•   the coast may be under threat but not economically valuable enough to save – money that may have been spent here may be better used in an area that has more need or is more valuable. *Note that a 'do nothing' approach might simply mean that the coast along these stretches is already well protected, either by natural or manmade defences, and therefore nothing further needs to be done. In this case, the benefits of the scheme are that time and money do not need to be spent defending these areas and can instead be focused on the areas that do need defending or managing. Here there are no real costs, as long as the initial appraisal of the state of the coastal defences has been done properly. There may also be environmental benefits of letting nature 'take its course' in terms of providing natural habitats for plants and animals. However, in other situations, the coast may be under very serious threat of erosion or flooding but it is not considered economically valuable enough to justify defending it. In this sort of case, the benefit remains that other areas that do have more reason to be defended can have attention and money focused on them, but there are then a wide range of costs that you can explore in your answer, as listed under 'Costs' above.*

54. River valleys

1   Rivers begin in upland areas and flow downhill. Near the source the long profile of a river shows a steep gradient. It gradually gets lower and less steep until the river reaches sea level. The river has a V-shaped cross profile in the upper course. By the time the river reaches its lower course, the valley is wide and flat.

2   (a) A V-shaped valley with narrow, shallow channel; C Wide, U-shaped valley with wide, deep channel and flat flood plain
(b) (i) B (ii) A (iii) C
The contour lines in diagram (ii) are very close together which indicates high land where all rivers start. Diagram (i) shows more tributaries are joining. It is still upland area but flatter than in A as the contours are further apart. Diagram

(iii) shows much flatter land as the contours are further apart. There is also evidence of meanders.

55. River processes

1   (a) Saltation
(b) When a river loses energy (slows down), it loses some of its ability to transport material. This slowing may happen when the river flows round an obstacle, or when discharge is reduced.

2   Both abrasion and attrition are forms of erosion but they erode material in different ways. Abrasion is the action of sandpapering on the banks and bed of the river. Attrition is where the rocks in the water hit against each other and become more rounded.

56. Erosion landforms

1   A Interlocking spur

2   (a) A Granite or hard rock/overhanging rock; B Plunge pool; C Gorge
(b) *You need to mention the process. The full sequence is needed. Example* A fault in the geology exposes layers of hard and soft rock. The hard rock, e.g. granite, overlies the soft rock; this is called the cap rock. Water pours over the drop, causing erosion of the softer underlying rock such as clay or sandstone. This leads to the development of a plunge pool. Overhanging harder rock eventually collapses into the plunge pool. Over time, the waterfall retreats towards the source, forming a steep-sided valley called a gorge.

57. Erosion and deposition landforms

1   Deposition

2   The deeper parts of the channel have the highest velocities. On Figure 2, the fastest velocity is 0.4 m/sec, which is on the deeper, outside bend.

58. Deposition landforms

1   The gradient of the river is at its lowest in the lower course of the river. This slows the velocity of the river down, which means that the river doesn't have enough energy to carry its load and is therefore forced to drop or deposit the sediment. The heaviest particles are dropped first, then the finer sediment later on. This can form landforms called deltas.

2   *See page 156 for answer.*

59. River landforms

1   (a) C Lower course
(b) Estuary *Other options: flood plain, meander*

2   (a) and (b) Your answers will depend on the river valley you have studied and the landform you have selected. *Don't forget to write the name of the river and major landform in the space provided – this is worth two marks.*

60. Flood risk factors

1   (a) The increase in discharge from the base flow level until it reaches peak discharge
(b) 2.5 hours
(c) 25 m³/sec
(d) River X is more likely to flood as it has a shorter lag time and higher discharge. This means more water arrives in the river more quickly. The channel is therefore more likely to fill up and overflow.

2   Impermeable rocks will not allow water to percolate into the rocks below the ground. The water then runs off into the river channel more quickly, causing a shorter lag time and a steep rising limb.

61. Hard engineering

1   (a) D Dam and reservoir
(b) The dam and reservoir store water through the year and then release it in a controlled way as required. This means the risk of flooding downstream is significantly reduced.
(c) *Example* People may have to move away from the construction area because the construction of a reservoir behind a dam requires a valley or valleys to be flooded. *Other options: cost of construction; sedimentation in*

*the reservoir (reducing its capacity) because
of the reduction in water velocity as it enters
the reservoir; landslides along the edge of the
reservoir due to erosion and slope instability;
a reduction in reservoir levels due to over-
abstraction; disruption to aquatic ecosystems –
fish breeding grounds.*

62. Soft engineering

1. (a) (ii) Soft engineering
   (iii) Soft engineering
   (b) There are different ways to answer this
   question. Remember that for questions like
   this, you should not write about disadvantages
   as well advantages. The Boscastle text
   extract does provide a way into the question
   because it describes the use of both hard and
   soft engineering responses, which is specific
   evidence. But you need to also use your
   understanding to explain why both types of
   strategy would have had advantages. For
   example, you could say that a soft engineering
   response like moving the car park would have
   been much cheaper than a hard engineering
   response to defend the car park and that, since
   cars are expensive and the Boscastle flooding
   involved many cars being swept away and badly
   damaged, moving the car park out of the flood
   risk zone is a very effective way of reducing the
   risk of this highly damaging problem occurring
   again. Boscastle also involved hard engineering
   strategies; for example, river widening and
   deepening. Here again you can use your
   understanding of rivers and flooding to answer
   the question. Widening and deepening rivers
   has advantages: the river can hold more water
   before it floods, which means Boscastle will not
   be as at risk of sudden flash flooding events.
   When a river flows through a town, hard
   engineering will be required in places to protect
   homes and businesses that cannot be rezoned.

63. Flood management

1. *Example* Social issue: Some areas might have
   hard engineering protection while others do
   not. Environmental issue: Hard engineering
   could create obstacles to fish migrations up the
   river. *Other options: Hard engineering could
   increase pollution from urban runoff into the river
   downstream of London. Soft engineering could
   involve planting more trees and creating more
   vegetation in London to reduce surface runoff.
   Note that environmental issues can include positive
   as well as negative impacts on the environment.*
2. Your answer will depend on the UK flood
   management scheme you have studied.
   *Remember to identify the name of the scheme as
   this is worth one mark. Make your explanation
   specific to the scheme you have studied: use
   details from that example rather than general
   statements that could apply anywhere.*

64. Glacial processes

1. (a) *See page 157 for answer.*
   (b) *See page 157 for answer.*
   (c) Bulldozing is when a glacier has retreated,
   leaving a pile of moraine where its snout has
   melted, and then advanced again, pushing the
   moraine away in front of it.

65. Erosion landforms 1

1. Snow in a mountainside hollow compacts into
   ice. Freeze-thaw weathering around the corrie
   means rock falls onto the ice. These rocks help
   the base of the corrie erode. A lip forms where
   the ice leaves the corrie because of rotational
   slip.
2. Two from: contours close together; contours
   curved round in a bowl shape; possibly a tarn;
   possibly a place name: cwm in Wales, cirque in
   the Alps (both mean corrie.
3. *See page 157 for answer.*

66. Erosion landforms 2

1. (a) *See page 157 for answer.*
   (b) *See page 157 for answer.*

67. Transportation and deposition landforms

1. (a) Lateral moraine
   (b) Landform Y probably formed when the
   glacier was wider than it is currently. Like X,
   landform Y is lateral moraine. It is formed by
   weathered rock and debris falling down the
   valley sides onto the glacier. The glacier must
   have then retreated and returned back up the
   valley as a smaller, narrower glacier. New lateral
   moraines were then formed alongside the now-
   narrower glacier, inside the old lateral moraines.
   The glacier is now retreating again, leaving both
   sets of lateral moraines behind.

68. Upland glaciated area

1. Evidence includes the following:
   - **Valley shape** The valley has steep sides and
   a wide, flat bottom: the classic 'U' shape of the
   glacial trough. This indicates glaciation because
   a glacier is a powerful eroding and transporting
   force that removes interlocking spurs of a river
   valley and deepens and broadens the valley as it
   passes through it.
   - **Waterfalls** The waterfalls at Dungeon Ghyll
   Force (grid reference 2906) and above it suggest
   a hanging valley. This valley probably had a
   smaller glacier in it that was formed in the
   corrie now occupied by Stickle Tarn (2807).
   This didn't erode as deeply as the main glacier
   in the Langdale Valley and so was left hanging
   higher up than the main valley floor.
   - **Misfit stream** The Great Langdale Beck
   looks much too small to be responsible for this
   deep, broad valley – this is also strong evidence
   of glaciation.

69. Activities and conflicts

1. *Example* Economic activity 1: Forestry could
   take place in this upland glaciated landscape:
   conifer trees could be grown for wood. Upland
   landscapes like this do not have fertile soil and
   not many people live there so it is a good place
   for growing trees. Economic activity 2: Tourism
   – hill walking in the dramatic glaciated upland
   landscape or watersports on the ribbon lakes
   formed by glaciation. *Other options: farming –
   upland sheep farming or lowland farming on the
   flat valley bottoms, where soils are more fertile;
   quarrying – upland glaciated areas can contain
   resistant rock types that are valuable for road
   building.*
2. Conservation means keeping natural habitats
   in upland glaciated areas but forestry usually
   means planting areas with fast-growing conifer
   trees that aren't the natural habitat – and then
   cutting them down again.

70. Tourism

1. Way 1: Footpath erosion from large numbers of
   visitors.
   Way 2, one from: disturbance to local wildlife;
   impacts from litter being dropped; impacts
   from vegetation being trampled.
2. Your answer will depend on the area you have
   studied. *Make sure you give the name of your
   example area. Depending on the area you've
   studied, management strategies might include
   footpath restoration, keeping tourists away from
   vulnerable areas (for example, recently re-seeded
   grassed areas) or introducing car parks outside
   popular tourist villages and towns to reduce
   congestion. Your management strategy should
   relate to your own example area, so use example-
   specific information to achieve this.*

71. Global urban change

1. The increase in the proportion of people living
   in towns and cities (urban areas)
2. (a) 47 per cent
   (b) **B** 46 per cent
   (c) In North America and Europe (HICs) the
   rate of urbanisation is projected to be slower,
   whereas in Africa and Asia (LICs, NEEs) the
   rate of urban growth is projected to increase.

72. Urbanisation factors

1. **C** A city with a population of more than
   10 million
2. Most of the megacities shown are in Asia, 12
   of the 21. Most are found in coastal locations.
   Many are found within the tropics. Paris is the
   only megacity in Europe.
3. *Example* Factor 1: High rates of rural–urban
   migration; Factor 2: Faster natural increase in
   cities (higher birth rate, lower death rate). *Other
   options: economic advantages concentrated in the
   cities; living conditions and opportunities greater in
   cities than rural areas.*

73. Non-UK city: location and growth

1. (a) Your answer will depend on your case study.
   *Remember to include the name of your city in
   the space provided: that will be worth one mark.
   Use compass directions to give accurate detail for
   your description (for example, Mumbai is located
   on the west coast of India, on India's Arabian Sea
   coastline).*
   (b) Your answer will depend on your case study.
   *Major cities are usually located on major trade
   routes, around important ports or in important
   agricultural or industrial regions.*
2. *Example* Reason 1: High natural increase occurs
   when birth rates are high and death rates are
   falling. One reason for this is that people in LICs
   and some NEEs still have large families because
   large families provide support for parents as
   they get older. Reason 2: Death rates in LICs
   and NEEs are decreasing due to improved
   medical care. Vaccinations and jabs, particularly
   for children, help prevent common diseases.
   *Other options: improved sanitation in city
   areas, reducing the spread of disease; improved
   education about sanitation and staying healthy.*

74. Non-UK city: opportunities

1. (a) The informal employment sector is
   when people work outside the control and
   supervision of the state; for example, someone
   sets up a street food stall and sells food to
   anyone who wants it. The street food seller does
   not pay taxes, does not get inspected to make
   sure they are preparing their food safely, and
   does not get any protection from the state.
   (b) First way: Urban growth has given people
   greater access to the sorts of services shared by
   communities, such as clean water supplies and
   proper sanitation. *Example* Second way: Large
   numbers of people living in cities means there
   is a large market for all sorts of services via the
   informal sector, which suits migrants. *Other
   options: social – access to financial services (e.g.
   loans); access to communication services (e.g.
   mobile phone networks); access to education
   services; access to energy supplies; economic –
   good places for industries to locate that rely on
   cheap labour.*

75. Non-UK city: challenges 1

1. **C** Rubbish is left by the roadside, which attracts
   rats.
   E Residents have to rely on open water sources
   for water and for sanitation, so they become
   very polluted.
2. *Example* Name of city: Mumbai, India.
   Rapid urban growth in LICs and NEEs
   means that many people coming to the city
   cannot find suitable housing, which leads to
   overcrowding in old, unsafe housing (slums) or
   people making shacks to live in on unoccupied
   bits of land in and around the city (squatter
   settlements). In Mumbai, the city's population
   has grown from 8 million in 1971 to an
   estimated 21 million in 2011. Mumbai is built
   on a peninsula, which restricts its growth. New
   migrants to the city often live on the streets, in
   slums and in squatter settlements. The largest
   squatter settlement is Dharavi, which was
   originally a rubbish tip. Now, over 1 million
   people live in 1 square mile. Homes are built
   out of whatever materials people can find, and
   are very cramped: the average self-built home
   is only 3.7 m by 3.7 m. Large families live

together in these cramped conditions, which is a challenging way to live. Water is rationed in Dharavi: it is turned on at 5.30 am for two hours, during which time everyone has to get all the water they need for the next day and night. Dharavi houses do not have toilets. On average, 500 people share each public latrine (toilet). The sewerage infrastructure is not well-maintained and there are frequent leaks; people also use patches of open ground as toilets. The sewage gets onto the streets and into water sources, spreading diseases like typhoid; there are 4000 cases of water-borne disease per day in Dharavi. *Other options: this example is about Dharavi. You should use a similar level of detail to describe the challenges of slums or squatter settlements in your LIC or NEE case study city.*

76. Non-UK city: challenges 2

1 (a) First problem: Almost half of the greenhouse gases emitted in Mexico City come from vehicles. This is linked to car congestion because emissions are increased when cars are stuck in slow-moving traffic jams. *Example* Second problem: Companies are having to use 42 per cent (on average) of their land for car parking for employees – land that they could be using to expand their business. *Other options: nearly 1000 people a year killed in traffic accidents; high costs in time for commuters (an average of 26 days a year spent on commuting) and money (an average of US$1700 a year on fuel and maintenance for their cars).*
(b) Your answers will depend in part on your case study. Ways include: improving the quality of bus services so that buses offer a much more convenient, pleasant and cheaper way of commuting than by car; investment in low-emission public transport technology (e.g. buses) for reducing greenhouse gas emissions; integrating transport services, so people can use one form of transport (e.g. bicycle) to reach a transport hub that can connect them directly to their place of work (e.g. by bus) or to another transport hub; congestion charges to make travelling by car into the city centre more expensive, with the funds raised used to improve public transport; introducing bus lanes and cycle lanes to make sure these transport methods are not delayed by traffic jams; private companies encouraged to join together to offer shuttle buses for employees. *Note: you do not have to know about the specific strategies actually used in Mexico City – just possible strategies.*

77. Planning for the urban poor

1 (a) First reason: The buildings in the unplanned neighbourhood are shown with large cracks in them. This suggests that the buildings were made from poor-quality materials or were built badly. Regeneration would replace or repair these buildings so they were not in danger of falling down. *Example* Second reason: Urban planning could improve waste collection services, which would reduce problems with pests and the spread of diseases and also improve the environmental quality of the neighbourhood. *Other options: improving sanitation so people's health would be less under threat; better road surfaces so vehicles can travel through the area, helping economic activities (businesses like the dairy could deliver products to more customers and more people would come to the area); regeneration of the urban environment (e.g. painting houses in attractive colours) would make it a more popular place to live; making it a safer environment (e.g. places to cross roads, better environmental quality) could reduce crime levels.*
(b) Two from: helps with identifying and prioritising the problems that have the biggest impact on people's lives; helps ensure that improvements will be used – sometimes with improvements imposed on people (top-down), people do not know how to use them or do not understand why they are improvements (e.g. toilet blocks can seem strange or unpleasant

for people used to using waste ground); reduces costs, because local people get involved in funding, fundraising and as volunteers to build, maintain and operate the scheme.

78. Urban UK

1 (i) Northern Scotland has a relatively low population density because its upland relief and colder climate make large areas hard to farm and live in. (ii) *Example* London has a relatively high population density because it is a global finance centre, creating many opportunities for high-paid jobs. *Other options: because it is located near to major markets in the European Union; because it has historically been a global centre for trade; because it is a capital city and offers the widest range of job opportunities in the UK.*

2 A Birmingham; C Leeds

3 Two from: physical factors – population densities are higher in areas with flatter relief and lower in areas with steeper relief, usually because flatter areas have been easier to farm and trade across in the past, compared to upland areas that are difficult to farm and difficult to travel across; economic factors – people have moved to the major cities of the UK, and to the south east of the UK, because this is where the best opportunities are for finding well-paid work in the largest range of jobs.

79. UK city: location and migration

1 (a) A Birmingham
(b) 1 per cent

2 Your answer will depend on your case study. *Possible impacts: the need to build more housing; changes in natural increase as a result of the age profile of international migrants; impacts on the economy, as cities with higher international immigration have stronger economic growth than those that do not.*

80. UK city: opportunities

1 (a) Increasing the number of plants in urban areas
(b) First way: Studies show that when roads are lined with trees, drivers slow down. This will reduce traffic noise and could reduce the number of traffic accidents (and how serious they are), and streets will feel safer for pedestrians. Second way: Trees and plants absorb carbon dioxide and release oxygen. This will reduce the city's greenhouse gas emissions, and could help reduce the impact of climate change on the city.

2 Your answer will depend on your case study. *Possible points: opportunities to improve health and fitness if green areas include new facilities for taking exercise, e.g. cycle lanes, parks, walks; opportunities to develop new skills and make friends/build communities if people volunteer to help out in community gardens.*

81. UK city: challenges 1

1 (a) Some people in cities do not have access to the same resources and opportunities as others.
(b) Feature 1: The most deprived areas (wards) are close to the centre of Birmingham (inner city) in areas like Washwood Heath, East Handsworth and Sparkbrook. *Example* Feature 2: The least deprived areas are in the northern wards of Birmingham (Sutton Four Oaks, Sutton New Hall). *Other option: there is a band of least deprivation in Edgbaston, on the outskirts of the inner city.*

2 Challenges could come from increased crime levels: these create challenges for people of (1) staying safe, (2) risk to their property from burglary and vandalism, (3) risks to their health and (4) employability if they take part in drug-taking or criminal activities. Urban deprivation also often means very low-quality and badly maintained housing, so people have to live in cold, damp and unsanitary housing, which can affect their physical and mental health. Often areas affected by urban deprivation have high rates of unemployment because there aren't many jobs there, so people are living on low incomes. This makes it challenging to buy

enough to eat, to eat healthy diets, or to provide opportunities for children in families (e.g. school trips).

82. UK city: challenges 2

1 (a) A 587219; B 587231
(b) First reason: Property prices in cities like London and Oxford can make it too expensive for people to buy or rent housing where they work. Cheaper property prices in a nearby town could be a reason for the development of a commuter settlement. Second reason: *Example* Bicester has excellent rail and motorway links to Birmingham, Oxford and London. Good transport links mean commuters can reach their place of work relatively quickly and reliably.
(c) One from: many young families; quiet in the daytime; congestion on roads and railways at rush hour; possibly dominated by schools; homes and retail outlets with other types of economic activity underrepresented; recent development of new housing estates and developments. Bicester could also start to experience urban sprawl as more people come to live there, which could impact on the surrounding countryside as the town expands.

83. UK urban regeneration

1 Your answer will depend on the urban regeneration example you have studied. *The best answers will show your thorough and detailed knowledge of your example and how you have understood what it is that makes an urban regeneration project effective. To evaluate effectiveness, your answer should look at the advantages and disadvantages of the project to explore how successful it has been. A good way to do this would be to look at the reasons why the urban regeneration project was needed, and then what the regeneration project did to address those needs. Just describing the problems of an urban area or the main features of the regeneration project will not produce a really successful answer.*

84. Sustainable urban living

1 (a) An energy meter means people can see how much the energy they are using is costing. This would encourage people to use less energy because they would be able to see how much money it was saving them. For example, people might not leave lights on, or leave mobile phone chargers permanently plugged in and switched on.
(b) Two from: a switch to LED street lighting, which provides the same amount of light as a traditional sodium street light (the yellow lights) but with half the power consumption; city transport systems such as geofencing, where hybrid buses (powered by electric and conventional fossil fuels) automatically switch to electric power when they enter city districts that currently suffer from high air pollution; reducing heat loss from older city buildings by adding insulation; offering lower taxes for lower energy use (and higher taxes for high energy use) to businesses and residents.

2 One from: fitting toilets which flush smaller volumes of water and washing machines that use less water; fitting shower heads that mix air with water to reduce water use without affecting the 'power shower' experience; increasing domestic storage of water (e.g. water butts to collect rainwater for garden use); fixing dripping taps; fixing leaks in water pipes; covering reservoirs (and swimming pools) to reduce loss of water through evaporation; education campaigns to encourage homes and businesses to reduce water waste; city laws that prevent the use of water for cleaning cars or watering gardens at certain times of day or on certain days; recycling water more, e.g. from domestic users to energy suppliers, or using domestic and business grey water to irrigate or water city green spaces.

85. Urban transport strategies

1 (a) **C** Peak time traffic congestion, as measured by vehicle speeds, is actually now worse than before the congestion charge was introduced; **E** Cycling in London has increased by 66 per cent since the introduction of the congestion charge.
(b) First way: People who drove short distances from their homes outside the congestion charge to work in central London would save a lot of money by cycling as bikes do not have to pay the congestion charge.
Second way: *Example* The money earned from the congestion charge each year is spent on transport for London, including new schemes to make cycling in London easier and more attractive. For example: the hire bicycles ('Boris bikes') that people can pick up and drop off at many locations around London; new cycle lanes and cycle paths, including new paths that cut through parks and green areas, saving time and also providing a pleasant route across central London; improved bike parks by train stations and bus stations so people can combine cycling and public transport.

86. Measuring development 1

1 (a) **C** Swaziland
(b) The relationship is a negative (inverse) one, so as income per head goes up, infant mortality rates come down.
(c) Options include: averages can conceal extreme highs and lows, so a figure like GDP per head can suggest a level of development that is not really true of the country as a whole; development is a complex subject and one measure only records one aspect (for example, income per head does not say anything about education levels or about the cultural richness of a country); there are difficulties in recording data from less developed countries, so a mix of measures may give a more accurate picture than just one; some measures are not very good because of changes in global development (for example, death rates are now low in almost all countries).

87. Measuring development 2

1 (a) **A** Of all the countries labelled in Figure 1, the Democratic Republic of Congo has the lowest Human Development Index (HDI) score; **C** There are no countries in the continent of Africa with HDI scores over 0.79.
(b) Figure 1 shows that, although there are rich countries in the global North, not all the countries in the north are rich. And in the global South there are richer countries as well as poorer ones. The Human Development Index is superior because it shows countries at different levels of development, taking into consideration individual differences between countries.

88. The Demographic Transition Model

1 (a) **A** Death **r**ate; **B** Birth rate; **C** Natural increase
(b) Reason 1: In stage 1, the birth rate is high because lack of effective medicine and sanitation means infant death rates are very high and people have lots of children because not many survive. Reason 2: *Example* In stage 2, although the death rate starts to fall because of increased availability of effective medical knowledge, people still continue to have lots of children because children are economically important (e.g. to farm family land). *Other options: children are needed to look after ageing parents in countries where there is little state support for old age; in stage 2, there may be few job opportunities or education opportunities for women and women's role may be seen as having and caring for children.*
(c) Two from: when women have jobs and careers they start to have children later and not so many children; families have fewer children once they can be sure that they will almost certainly all survive; family planning

becomes available; female education becomes available; governments bring in birth reduction programmes.

89. Uneven development: causes

1 (a) Physical
(b) *Example* The charity advert says that it takes two hours for Kwame to get water from the waterhole. This means he has no time to go to school in the dry season. If Kwame does not complete his education he has less chance of getting a better job when he is older. This will affect his standard of living considerably. The same is true for many women and children in Ghana who spend most of their dry-season days fetching water. There is no time for the women to attend agricultural school to learn about making their crops grow better, so they cannot earn extra from farming, which again affects standards of living right across the country. When Kwame is sick from drinking unsafe water, he cannot help on the family farm. If he gets really ill, his parents have to pay for him to see a doctor and pay for the medicine. When a family has so little money, these sorts of expenses can affect their income for the whole year. If Kwame's parents get ill, then they cannot work and this can also be very serious for standards of living.

90. Uneven development: consequences

1 (a) People from poorer countries can earn more working in richer countries, so people have come to live and work in Peterborough from poorer countries to make better lives there.
(b) Two from: economic development – studies show that cities that are popular destinations for international migration have faster-growing economies than cities that are less popular with international migrants; increased diversity in the city meaning more choice of restaurants and entertainment; an increase in the labour force for employers (for example, in the food processing industries, which need a lot of workers prepared to work for low wages); problems between different ethnic groups. *You could also use the impact described in Figure 1, but put it into your own words.*
(c) Uneven development means that some countries are much poorer than others. International migration is a consequence of this situation because those who are able to make the journey can travel to find work in richer countries, and then send home money to help their families.

91. Investment, industry and aid

1 (a) **C** India
(b) The countries that donate the most are all high-income, industrialised countries in western Europe, North America and Australia. The countries that receive the most are concentrated in west Africa and south-eastern Europe, and in more scattered locations in central and south-east Asia and in parts of South America.
2 Advantages include: when aid is targeted at the poorest people in a country, especially on large-scale education or health improvements, it can have a huge impact on development because national governments do not always have the resources and expertise to carry out these big social programmes. Disadvantages include: sometimes aid is tied to the country buying products or services from the receiving country, which may not offer value for money or the best solution for that country; international aid is sometimes siphoned off due to corruption so it does not reach the poorest people it is designed to help; sometimes aid is used inefficiently or wastefully on projects that will actually do very little to reduce the development gap; some say international aid encourages receiving countries to depend on aid rather than focus on meeting their development needs for themselves.

92. Technology, trade, relief and loans

1 (a) £208 million (2011) − £16 million (2001) = £192 million
(b) Sales initially increased gradually: from £15 to £65 million (£50 million) between 2001 and 2006. Between 2006 and 2007, sales increased significantly, jumping from £65 million to £150 million: an increase of 130 per cent. Following that, growth slowed slightly, with sales reaching £200 million in the last months of 2008. After a peak of sales in 2009, there was a slight decline in 2010 with sales then appearing to flatten out at just over the £200 million per year mark.
(c) Possible points: schemes that offer a minimum price to cover costs even when world prices fall; schemes that include a premium on the price which is then invested back into community projects; schemes that bring producers together so they have more strength to resist price-cutting measures.

93. Tourism

1 (a) Beach holidays and wildlife safari holidays
(b) Reason 1: More places for tourists to visit would mean more tourists visiting Kenya. When tourists come from countries like China, Russia, the UK and the USA, they pay for their trips in foreign currency, which is worth a lot in Kenya. This money is very important to the national economy. Reason 2: Spreading tourism out over more areas in Kenya will mean more Kenyan people can benefit economically, not just from jobs in tourist centres, but also, for example, by making handicraft products to sell to tourists. This would help reduce the development gap regionally as well as nationally.
2 Your answer will depend on the example you have studied. *Your answer should consider to what extent the economic benefits of tourism have spread beyond the popular resorts and into the wider economy, through multiplier effects. So, for example, direct employment created in tourist resorts may also have been accompanied by an increase in the amount of indirect employment created in industries that supply the tourist resorts, such as craft industries that produce goods sold as souvenirs to tourists, farms that supply resorts with food, and coach and taxi services which transport tourists around the country. Try to add detail to your answer; for example, the contribution of tourism to your example country's economy.*

94. LIC or NEE country: location and context

1 Your answer will depend on your case study. *Make sure you include the name of your case study country as this is worth a mark.*
2 Your answer will depend on your case study. *For a strong answer, include detail to support the feature you describe.*
3 Your answer will depend on your case study. *Vague answers that could apply to any LIC or NEE will not be as successful as answers that apply accurate and relevant detail specific to your case study.*

95. LIC or NEE country: TNCs

1 Your answer will depend on your case study. Common advantages include:
• increased income for the government from taxation
• development of mineral resources
• provision of infrastructure
• more employment opportunities
• more services
• development of skills for local people
• more money in local economies.
Common disadvantages include:
• low wages
• poor working conditions (e.g. long hours)
• raw materials are extracted in the host country, but sent elsewhere for processing, so limiting the development of other local industries based on those raw materials

- profits being taken away, out of the host country
- environmental issues of pollution, contamination and over-use of resources (e.g. groundwater)
- withdrawal of a TNC from a host country leaving people stranded without jobs.
Make sure you include specific examples from your case study country.

96. LIC or NEE country: trade, politics and aid

1 (a) **C** Western Europe
  (b) 500 billion dollars
2 Your answer will depend on your case study. *Ideally, give specific information about increases in the value of global trade following the opening up of your LIC or NEE to global trade. Remember to link this increase to economic development of the country.*

97. LIC or NEE country: environmental impact

1 Your answer should consider points for and against the statement.
  Possible points in favour:
  - Good quality of life means a good standard of living and an increased opportunity for people to live comfortable and healthy lives. Economic development is the main reason for increased quality of life.
  - Economic development has helped lift millions of people out of poverty, especially in China following China's rapid industrialisation at the end of the 20th century.
  - Economic development usually involves people leaving subsistence agriculture for jobs in the industrial cities. Subsistence agriculture is a hard way of life: the work is very hard for very little money, people live in poor housing with poor food, there are limited health and education services and few things they can afford to buy. Quality of life is far better in cities.
  - Economic development creates jobs, which mean people have money to spend. People with money to spend buy more products, which increases economic development and creates more and better-paid jobs. People have more money and more things, which usually means better quality of life.
  Possible points against:
  - Although China has seen millions lifted out of poverty, this is not due to economic development alone. Without a government committed to sharing wealth, to some extent, among its people, China could have seen the rise of an elite of very wealthy people while the majority of the population remained very poor.
  - Although quality of life is higher in NEE cities than in NEE subsistence agriculture, the sorts of jobs open to most rural migrants in LICs and NEEs are often still dirty, sometimes dangerous, extremely tedious, low paid and low status. Education and health services may be available, but perhaps only at a high cost. If they are free or cheap to urban workers, this is not because of economic development but because of government intervention to make them free or cheap.
  - Often people have to make significant sacrifices to find better jobs. Men have to leave their families and get jobs in far-off cities or other countries. Parents have to leave young children back in the home village with grandparents. City life is full of stress and pressure. People's income may rise, but that does not necessarily mean an increase in quality of life.

98. UK: deindustrialisation, globalisation and policy

1 **C** Rapid decline in employment was matched by a similar drop in coal output
2 Reason 1: Globalisation has meant that coal can be imported into the UK from countries where it can be mined much more cheaply, so

even though it has to be shipped to the UK, it is still cheaper for UK industries to buy coal than to mine it in the UK. *Example Reason 2:* There was less demand for coal in the UK, e.g. in power stations, as they began to switch to cleaner alternatives, such as gas. *Other option: less demand for coal in the UK as heavy industries (that used a lot of coal) began to decline.*

99. UK: post-industrial economy

1 (a) **D** 1990–2010
  (b) *Example* One reason is the decline in heavy industry and manufacturing in the UK, because as jobs in these industries have shifted from the UK to cheaper locations in other parts of the world, service sector jobs have replaced them. *Other options: an increase in productivity in industry and agriculture so that fewer people are now required to do those jobs; more people having better standards of living and being able to afford to use more services; companies outsourcing service parts of their operations to other companies (e.g. car manufacturers outsourcing marketing, car cleaning or car maintenance); the importance of banking and financial services to the UK economy (so this sector has grown very big in the UK); or similar explanations.*
2 You can use evidence from the example of sustainable modern industry that you have studied. *As well as evidence details, you need to use your points to support the statement. Do not just **describe** the example you have studied; make sure you **explain** how its practices are environmentally sustainable. You could conclude that if some industries have found ways to become more sustainable, there is potential for all industries to do so, too.*

100. UK: rural change

1 (a) The average wage in Herefordshire is over £5100 less per year than the average wage for England, and over £7100 less per year than the average wage in urban areas of England. This is important for understanding rural depopulation because people will move to other parts of the UK to get a wider range of better-paid jobs with better career prospects.
  (b) *Example* An increasing number of people depend on the internet for entertainment and remote working. As this requires a broadband connection or mobile phone network, rural areas without these services would not be attractive to these people. *Other options: A lack of affordable housing makes it difficult for young people to continue to live in the area once they have left their parents' homes because they can't afford to rent or buy flats or houses of their own. There is little help for parents with young children – when people have children they need to have health and child care services around them. Babies need regular health and development checks (and seem to get ill a lot) and, if both parents are working, there need to be childminding services to look after the young children. Both of these types of service are common in urban areas, but generally are more difficult to access in rural areas.*

101. UK: developments

1 (a) The top three regions for economic output per person are all in the south of the UK, which supports the idea of a divide between the south and the north of the UK.
  (b) Two from the following:
  - London has a finance industry that generates enormous income for the UK and for the people who work in it.
  - London is a major centre for global companies, which create a lot of well-paid jobs.
  - London is very popular as a global tourist centre.
  - People make a lot of money from buying and selling property in London. Houses are worth far more in London and parts of the south-east because there are not enough houses for all the people who want to work in London.

- So many people live in London and the south-east that it is a huge market for retailers: people who sell things in shops make a lot of money from shoppers in London and the south.

102. UK and the wider world

1 (a) **C** European Union
  (b) 46.7 (to 1 decimal place)
  (c) Advantage: The European Union is the world's biggest single market and a very important market for UK products: in 2016, around 45 per cent of the UK's trade was with the EU. *Example* Disadvantage: Trading with the EU if you are not an EU member involves paying tariffs: these mean that UK firms earn less money from their exports than their competitors within the EU. *Other options: Some countries have agreed trade deals with the EU that do not involve high tariffs, but which involve accepting the right of people from across the EU to live and work in the other country. This has led to concerns over immigration in some countries. By focusing on trading with the EU, UK businesses could be missing out on opportunities to trade with other countries.*

103. Essential resources

1 (a) In numerical order: 10, 14, 34, 43, 88, 100; two middle numbers: 34, 43. Median: $77 \div 2 = 38.5$
  (b) Consumption increases with development. As economies become more developed their industries use more resources. As their people become wealthier, they consume more products, use more energy, use more water, and eat more and a greater variety of food.
  (c) Economic wellbeing relates to the ways that having more money can make life easier and better; for example, having a job means being able to buy enough food for your family all week. Social wellbeing is about the extent to which you feel part of your communities and connected to the people around you; having good relationships with your family and friends, for example.

104. UK food resources

1 (a) **A** Pie chart; **C** Bar chart
  (b) Costa Rica's tropical climate gives it a significant advantage over the UK for producing fresh fruit all year because it is much warmer than the UK's climate. Costa Rica is able to continue to grow fresh fruit throughout the year as it does not have a winter like the UK's, where there is not enough energy being received from the Sun for plants to grow well.
2 *Example* Because the UK wants to have year-round access to fruit that is only grown seasonally in the UK, such as apples, in some months retailers will import this fruit from other countries, such as Spain. Other fruit – including the UK's most popular fresh fruit, the banana – cannot be grown in the UK at all and is imported from countries like Costa Rica and Columbia. Transporting the fruit to the UK involves high carbon emissions, which has environmental impacts in terms of climate change. *Other point: if UK producers were to use technology to grow fruit all year to meet the UK all-year demand, this would also lead to high carbon emissions as heated greenhouses would have to be used and generating the heat is very energy-intensive.*

105. UK water resources

1 (a) **D** The north
  (b) Reason 1: In the UK, precipitation is much higher in the north and west than in the south and east, so there is usually water surplus in the north and west, while the south and east can experience water deficit. Reason 2: Because the population density of the south and east of the UK is higher than the north and west, there is higher demand in the south and east for water.
  (c) *Example* There are high carbon emissions involved in construction and in pumping water up gradients, as water is extremely heavy

and requires a lot of energy to move against gravity. *Other options: high cost of building such schemes; environmental problems caused by moving water from one region to another – water from different drainage basins has different chemical properties, which can be toxic to freshwater organisms that are not adapted to it (a water quality issue); large-scale water transfer projects in other countries have also experienced major problems with pollution – as water is moved through the countryside it picks up pollution from agricultural runoff so that by the time a lot of water has been moved a long way it can have higher pollution levels as a result.*

106. UK energy resources

1 **A** Coal had the biggest drop of all the energy resources in terms of its share in UK electricity generation; **B** The biggest increase in share of electricity generation was in renewables, not nuclear.

2 The range of energy resources of a country or region. The energy mix can be made up of either renewable or non-renewable resources or a mixture of the two.

3 Reason 2: In order to reduce greenhouse emissions, the UK's energy mix now includes <u>renewable sources of energy such as onshore and offshore wind and solar, as well as nuclear power</u>.

107. Demand for food

1 **C** The world saw a larger increase in food consumption per person between 1974 and 2015 than the industrialised countries on their own, but this global increase was smaller than the increase for developing countries.

2 Two from: climate, technology, pests, disease, water stress, conflict, poverty.

3 (a) When the majority of the population of an LIC farms land to feed themselves (subsistence agriculture), food consumption is low and is mostly made up of one or two plant crops. When people leave rural areas to work in industry in cities, <u>they earn more money and can afford to eat more food, and a greater variety of food.</u> (b) *Example* The more people there are, the more food in total the population will eat.

108. Food insecurity

1 *Example* Food insecurity is a lack of reliable access to enough safe, nutritious food. <u>One impact of food insecurity is famine. Famines, which are rare, are defined as occurring when at least 20 per cent of households in an area face extreme food shortages, when more than 30 per cent of people are acutely malnourished and when more than two people per day per 10 000 people are dying. For example, a famine in Ethiopia in 1983–1985 led to 400 000 deaths: although drought was a factor in this famine, the major cause was civil war.
Undernutrition is a second impact of food insecurity. Undernutrition results from not having enough to eat and it causes children to be underweight and too short for their age. It also means that people do not have enough energy to work productively enough vitamins and minerals in their diets to stay healthy, so undernutrition is also linked to people being frequently ill. This can affect their ability to work and earn money, and for children it means they miss out on school.
A third impact of food insecurity is soil erosion because people are pushed by food insecurity to try to find new places to grow crops or get more food out of the land that they have. Over-using soil means the soil becomes unstructured and loses its organic content, which makes it much easier for wind and water to erode. Farming in marginal areas also encourages soil erosion because this marginal land is already very low in nutrients and organic material.</u> *Other impacts listed in the specification are rising prices and social unrest. Your answer does not need to cover all of them but the ones you do discuss should be*

covered in detail. Note, too, that the definitions of some of the impacts (like famine) are important because they refer to precise, specific conditions.

109. Increasing food supply

1 (a) Method A: Aeroponics; Method B: <u>Hydroponics</u>
(b) *Example* The supply of nutrients can be carefully controlled to optimise the plants' growth and development. *Other options: the water is recycled; the water does not drain down into soil; there are no weeds so all the nutrients supplied go directly to the plants; pests cannot get in to eat the plants; because the plants are under controlled conditions it is much easier to control the spread of plant diseases; because soil is not required the plants can be grown anywhere, including in cities.*

2 (a) Appropriate technology is technology at the right level to be useful and accessible to the communities who are using it.
(b) *Example* If water stress is an issue for a community, appropriate technology can provide opportunities to increase water storage in the community, and ways to increase the amount of water stored in the soil or in river beds during the dry season. If soil erosion is an issue, appropriate technology can provide strategies for the community to use to protect the soil, such as bunds or grass strips between farmed strips. Poverty can be reduced by providing communities with appropriate technology to process crops into more valuable products, such as the Universal Nut Sheller. *Note that this is a good opportunity to use an example to add detail to your answer.*

110. Sustainable food supplies

1 (a) **C** Farming that follows the way that natural ecosystems work
(b) Growing food in cities reduces the distance that food has to be transported to be available to urban populations. This helps make food supply more sustainable because <u>transportation of food means increased carbon emissions and increased use of non-renewable resources for fuel for transportation.</u>
(c) First way: Getting meat and fish from sustainable sources
Example Second way: <u>Using organic farming methods.</u> *Other options: permaculture; seasonal food consumption; reducing food waste; reducing food loss.*

2 Your answer will depend to some extent on the example you studied in class. Ways in which local schemes can increase sustainable supplies of food include:
• benefitting from government agricultural research projects and non-governmental organisations' research and expertise
• increasing water supplies through rainwater harvesting or dams
• improving water quality by filtering it through sand or reed beds
• education for local farmers on ways to improve yields in sustainable ways (e.g. through composting, mixed agriculture where the manure from livestock is used to maintain soil nutrient levels, techniques like rice-fish farming where fish are farmed in the water-filled rice paddies – with the fish eating pests and providing fertiliser through their excrement, and also providing a source of protein for the farmers)
• reforesting slopes and growing trees among crops (agroforestry) to act as wind breaks, stabilise the soil and increase biodiversity
• growing a mixture of crops (e.g. maize and beans) to provide nitrogen-fixing for the soil
• providing land plots for homeless and landless people and families, slowing rural–urban migration.

111. Demand for water

1 **B** Most of Africa has a water deficit; **E** Most regions along the Equator have a water surplus.

2 Two from: climate, geology, pollution of supply, over-abstraction, limited infrastructure, poverty.

3 (a) As a country industrialises, water consumption increases significantly because heavy industry and power generation require <u>large amounts of water for cooling, and in industry for many other aspects of manufacture.</u>
(b) The more people there are, the more water in total the population will require for drinking, washing and growing crops.

112. Water insecurity

1 Water security is about people having reliable access to enough safe water for them to have a healthy and productive life, and about reducing the risk of water hazards. <u>One impact of water insecurity is waterborne disease. Each year it is estimated that over 3 million people die because of diseases spread in water such as typhoid and dysentery – 900 children a day. As well as deaths, waterborne diseases make millions of people very ill, so they cannot work or go to school. These diseases are preventable by improving sanitation, but currently 650 million people in the world do not have access to safe water. Such huge health impacts from waterborne disease makes development much harder to achieve.
A second impact of water insecurity is on food production. Agriculture uses 70 per cent of water worldwide – it takes a lot of water to grow crops and even more to raise animals for meat and milk. Water insecurity can affect farmers because of long droughts, especially in regions where farmers rely on rain to provide the water their crops need, and also if water supplies are polluted so they cannot be used for crops. When farmers cannot get enough water for their crops, food insecurity can become a problem. Conflict can result over the management of water in regions where there is water insecurity, especially over the management of rivers that flow through more than one country.</u> *Other impacts in the specification are: water pollution, industrial output and the potential for conflict where demand exceeds supply. Your answer does not need to cover all of them but the ones you do discuss should be covered in detail.*

113. Increasing water supply

1 (a) Desalination
(b) Because 97 per cent of the Earth's water is in the sea and therefore too saline for drinking, growing crops or many other uses, <u>the big advantage of desalination is that it creates freshwater out of seawater or other sources of brackish water (e.g. some lakes, lagoons).</u>

2 (a) Other strategies: diverting supplies of water and increasing storage; dams and reservoirs and water transfers.
(b) If you used information from your large-scale water transfer scheme to answer this question, you might have included as advantages: ability to transfer water from areas of surplus to areas of deficit; opportunity to increase agricultural and industrial production in currently water-insecure areas and also for urbanisation; water no longer needing to be diverted from farming to meet industrial needs or domestic needs. Disadvantages include: cost (e.g. the South to North Water Transfer Project in China has an estimated cost of $62 billion); social impacts of relocating people in the way of the scheme; environmental impacts from increased pollution of the transferred water; wasteful nature of water transfers in which large volumes of water are lost to evaporation.

114. Sustainable water supplies

1 (a) **B** Reusing water that has been used by homes and businesses for other purposes, e.g. cooling in industry
(b) Recycling water means using 'grey water' (water that has already been used for one purpose) to meet other needs – so, for example,

water used in homes is then recycled for watering grass or as a coolant in industry. This helps make water supply more sustainable because it is using the same water twice, reducing the amount of water that needs to be abstracted.
(c) Way 1: Groundwater management
Way 2: Water conservation

2 Your answer will depend on the example you have studied. Common ways include:
- increasing water supply by collecting more rainwater – for example, using appropriate technology
- increasing water supply by storing more rainwater – for example, underground storage tanks
- increasing water supply by installing low concrete dams (sand dams) in river beds (in the dry season) or stream beds on hillsides to create mini reservoirs; the low river dams trap sand and sediment behind them, water sinks into these deposits and is stored there for use in the dry season; the sand also filters the water, making it safer to use
- small-scale water transfer schemes to pipe water from wetter upland regions or upland springs to drier valleys where people farm – using gravity rather than fossil-fuel-powered pumps is more sustainable
- increasing water supply by digging irrigation ditches linked to bunds – mini dams put into rivers in the wet season channel water down irrigation ditches to one group of fields; the bund is then moved downstream to the next channel and set of fields
- increasing water conservation – for example, introducing appropriate technology drip irrigation systems, and installing covers on wells and storage tanks to reduce evaporation
- increasing understanding of rainfall measurement – when farmers measure rainfall it enables them to recognise the best times to plant crops, and which crops to plant
- putting water management schemes into the hands of local communities – communities then manage them to meet their needs and do necessary repairs and maintenance.

115. Demand for energy

1 **D** By 2025, energy consumption in China is predicted to be approximately 10 times its consumption in 1990.

2 Two from: physical factors, cost of exploitation and production, technology and political factors.

3 (a) When the majority of the population are subsistence farmers, energy consumption is low: people use wood as fuel, and human and animal muscle power to work their fields. When people leave rural areas to work in industry in cities, their energy consumption increases as they earn more, improve their living conditions with domestic appliances (air conditioning, ovens, hot water) and use motor transport to get to work.
(b) The more people there are, the more energy in total the population will require for heating (and cooling), leisure and communications, transportation and work.

116. Energy insecurity

1 Energy security is about people and industries having reliable access to enough energy at affordable prices. One impact of energy insecurity is that areas where energy extraction was previously considered too difficult may become viable either because of increases in the price of energy or because the countries that own these areas want to increase the security of their energy supply. This is the case with deepwater oil drilling, for example: it is technically very difficult but countries and companies will take the risk in order to increase their energy security. Environmentally sensitive areas can be impacted by the exploration for fossil fuels that comes with energy insecurity – fracking is a good example. This is a method

that has made the extraction of gas from shale rocks a commercially viable process, but the method is thought to have potentially damaging environmental impacts, which could have serious environmental consequences for areas other people prize for their natural beauty.
A second impact of energy insecurity is industrial output. Some industries require large amounts of energy – a good example is steel production. Large steel companies owned by TNCs will decide on the location of steelworks at least in part based on the cost of electricity. So rising prices for electricity, due to energy insecurity, may become a reason why the TNC switches location of steel production to other parts of the world; for example in Brazil where large HEP projects provide a reliable source of cheap electricity. *Other impacts listed in the specification are economic and environmental costs, food production and the potential for conflict where demand exceeds supply. Your answer does not need to cover all of them but the ones you do discuss should be covered in detail.*

117. Increasing energy supply

1 (a) Solar
(b) During daylight hours, around 173 000 terawatts of solar energy reaches the Earth's surface, which is around 12 000 times more energy than is currently consumed by all humans in a year. The Sun provides a huge, free and entirely renewable source of energy every day.

2 Your answer will depend on the example you have studied.
Advantages could include one from the following:
- If a country has sizeable fossil fuel deposits then this increases the country's energy security. For example, the UK's North Sea oil and gas reduced the UK's dependence on foreign energy suppliers.
- Fossil fuels can mean that a country is able to export energy to other countries. For some fossil-fuel-rich countries this is what the majority of their economic development depends on.
- Fossil fuels are very effective sources of power and allow both agricultural and industrial development.
- Fossil fuel extraction creates a lot of jobs: in 2016, 450 000 UK jobs were directly in North Sea oil and gas or in industries linked to it.
- Although some fossil fuels are heavy polluters and carbon emitters, some are cleaner than others. Natural gas, for example, produces 45 per cent less carbon dioxide than coal.
Disadvantages could include one from the following:
- Burning fossil fuels releases carbon dioxide into the atmosphere: a greenhouse gas.
- Fossil fuels eventually run out. The UK's reserves in the North Sea reached peak production in 1999: production will now gradually decline.
- Fossil fuel prices drive the world economy and a fall in prices can hit the economic development of oil-exporting countries very hard.
- Extracting fossil fuels is dangerous work and the risk of accidents needs to be carefully monitored. Accidents can kill workers and can also cause very significant environmental disasters such as oil spills. In 2010, the Deepwater Horizon oil disaster in the Gulf of Mexico killed 11 people and released 4.9 million barrels of oil into the marine ecosystem of the Gulf of Mexico. The oil company, BP, had to pay US$18 billion in fines because of the environmental damage caused.
- Most countries have signed up to treaties committing them to lowering carbon emissions. To do this, countries have to reduce their reliance on fossil fuels and increase their use of alternative, sustainable energy sources.

118. Sustainable energy supplies

1 Because hydrogen does not emit any CO_2 when used as a fuel, using hydrogen buses for public transport will reduce an area's carbon footprint because of all the CO_2 emissions CO_2 of that are no longer being produced by using fossil fuels to power buses.

2 Your answer will depend on the example you have studied.
Example LIC or NEE local renewable energy schemes often involve run-of-river micro-hydro. Benefit 1: If NGOs and the government help in building the micro-hydro and local people are trained in operating and maintaining the micro-hydro plant, then running and repairing a micro-hydro scheme is generally low cost; something the community can afford to run. Benefit 2: The whole community is able to benefit from the electricity generated by the scheme. Homes have heat in the winter and light at night-time, people can have televisions and refrigerators. New industries can be set up, helping the economic development of the community. *Other schemes: solar power mini grids; local biomass schemes. Other benefits: creation of jobs and development of skills; benefits for education as children can study at night; benefits for the community in helping to keep people in the community rather than leaving to live in the cities. Rather than describing the scheme, focus on identifying two benefits for communities and explaining why they are benefits.*

119. Working with a resource booklet

1 6-mark questions like this are marked by levels.
- Level 1 is for basic answers: 1–2 marks. These answers only show limited understanding and application. For this question, a basic answer might only list some negative factors and not make any valid reference to Figures 1 and 2.
- Level 2 is for clear answers: 3–4 marks. These answers would show a good understanding of a range of ways in which energy development impacts on the tropical rainforest, both positive and negative, and would use evidence from Figures 1 and 2 as support.
- Level 3 is for detailed answers: 5–6 marks. As well as communicating ideas clearly, these answers would use detail to support an evaluation of the issues involved, weighing up the problems and benefits with reference to relevant information from Figures 1 and 2, and then come to a supported conclusion.

120. Contemporary geographical issues

1 Benefit: Migrant workers would benefit because they would get a job and earn money from working on the construction of the dam. Disadvantage: People could be forced to move away from the area (40 000 people forced to move – info from Figure 1). *Other options: large-scale HEP requires reservoirs which flood wide areas (own understanding); loss of traditions for indigenous peoples forced to change their ways of life in the area; loss of livelihoods from people who depend on local fish species, which might become endangered as a result of the dam.*

121. Evaluating issues

1 The balance of the case you make will vary according to the project you choose. Here are some key points.
- **Project 1 Build the Belo Monte dam and further HEP schemes to produce more HEP.** Brazil's long-term economic development will depend on the development of energy resources. HEP is a clean, green energy source that will not contribute to global warming. It is also a finite energy resource that will not run out. Development of the dam will create skilled jobs for local people and migrant workers, which will boost the local economy and the quality of life for people in the area. There are environmental concerns with this project, such as

as the flooding of large areas of rainforest, interrupting the flow of the river and disturbing aquatic ecosystems. With careful planning and management, many of these concerns can be addressed.
• **Project 2 Make the area a national park and increase the amount of energy produced from biogas.** Local and global resources from the tropical rainforest will be conserved for the long term. This would mean that the rainforest resources could not be used for commercial benefit, which could hinder economic growth in Brazil. However, the national park could attract tourists, which could help boost the local economy. Developing biogas is a sustainable project – it is a carbon-neutral fuel. The local climate and environment are suited to growing the crops needed, and there is sufficient space in Brazil to do this.
• **Project 3 Develop smaller HEP dams, and solar and wind power.** This is a more bottom-up approach, which might mean less local opposition and less damage to the environment compared with the top-down mega dam project. Solar power may not be very efficient in some cloudy parts of the rainforest. Large areas of rainforest would have to be cleared to make way for solar farms. Wind farms may not be suitable deep in the sheltered rainforest regions, which contain dense vegetation. Development may be slower but more sustainable, as solar power, wind power and HEP do not emit any greenhouse gases and will not be finite in supply.

122. Enquiry questions
1 The car park is full so there would be plenty of visitors to <u>answer questionnaires or take part in other surveys.</u>
2 Your answer will depend on your own human fieldwork enquiry. *In your answer, you need to state two advantages and then explain each advantage. Possible advantages: accessibility (how easy the location is to get to); safety considerations (e.g. whether there is a pavement along the roadside); whether there is a range of survey points available. Example* With a range of survey points, it was possible to measure the change in numbers of people away from the car park location.

123. Selecting, measuring and recording data
1 Options for coastal area: beach profiles, sediment analysis, measuring longshore drift, sand dune sampling, (also tourism fieldwork questions). Options for urban area: traffic counts, pedestrian counts, environmental quality surveys, land use mapping, building heights, photographs, field sketches.
2 Your answer will depend on the primary data collection method you used in your own human geography enquiry. *Justification options: why the method is accurate or reliable; why it was appropriate in terms of the theory or concept being tested; why the way your survey or questionnaire questions were written was appropriate for your enquiry.*

124. Processing and presenting data
1 A cross-sectional diagram
2 (a) Scattergraphs can only be used to show relationships between two variables, so are inappropriate here as there are three sets of data.
(b) A histogram, because each bar of a histogram is used for a <u>range of data (e.g. 5–14) rather than a specific category like a bar chart.</u>

125. Analysing data and reaching conclusions
1 Your answer will depend on the analysis that you did for your physical geography fieldwork enquiry.
• 6-mark questions are marked according to levels, with 1–2 marks for a basic answer, 3–4 marks for a clear answer and 5–6 marks for a detailed answer, so make sure you add detail.
• Analysing data is often about recognising

patterns and trends, identifying relationships between variables and spotting things that don't fit the trend – anomalies.
• It is absolutely valid to talk about problems with collecting data or with getting enough data to be representative.
• The question does ask about a reliable conclusion, so your answer should relate directly to whether or not your analysis helped or didn't help the reliability of your conclusion. This is where you can use your knowledge of strengths and limitations of your methods of analysis.

126. Evaluating geographical enquiries
1 (a) **B** Students C and D are both evaluating the appropriateness of their river fieldwork sample sites; **C** Students A and E are both evaluating the reliability of their data collection methods.
(b) An alternative way of measuring river velocity is a flow meter. This has a mechanism which revolves in the flow of water, recording each revolution. This would be more accurate than the float method because <u>the flow meter is not impeded by bedload in the way that the float method is.</u>
(c) Your answer will depend on the data collection methods you used in your own physical geography enquiry.

127. 6-mark questions
1 *Example:* Extreme weather is when weather conditions are significantly different from the average weather patterns. If weather is becoming more extreme in the UK, this would mean not only that individual weather events are extreme, but that there is an increasing number of these extreme events.
<u>Figure 1 talks about flood defences built only a few years ago, in 2012, that the Storm Desmond floods went straight over the top of. It also talks about people in Keswick being flooded three times. This is evidence of weather becoming more extreme in the UK because the 2012 flood defences would have been built high enough to contain expected flood levels. Just three years later, in 2015, Storm Desmond's flooding was already higher than the flood defences. The fact that people in Keswick had already been flooded three times suggests that this type of extreme weather is increasing – if it wasn't increasing then, no one would be surprised that flooding was this common.</u>
<u>Figure 1 mentions that 130 flood warnings were in place and that torrential rain affected large parts of northern England and Scotland in December 2015. This extreme weather is not a one-off, however: the winter of 2013/14 was the wettest since 1910.</u>

128. 9-mark questions
1 *Example*: Economic development does have many positive effects on quality of life for people in LICs and NEEs. Quality of life in rural settlements is very low: people work very hard for very little money, there are few services and low levels of education and healthcare. This is why rural–urban migration is so high in LICs and NEEs: <u>cities offer far better opportunities to earn more money and access a much wider range of services. The rapid economic development of cities provides more jobs, more services and more opportunities. Mexico City, for example, now has 6–7 per cent of Mexico's population and produces one quarter of Mexico's national wealth. In the cities, even if people only get informal sector work, then quality of life can be higher and they can earn more money than before. They may not have to pay as much rent. There are more opportunities for education and for healthcare, although these may be expensive.</u> However, I do not agree that economic development only has positive effects on people's quality of life. In fact, the rapid economic growth of LIC and NEE cities has usually meant that <u>quality of life suffers as the city's population</u>

grows faster than housing, employment and services can keep up with. In Mexico City, for example, it is estimated that 60 per cent of jobs are in the informal sector. This has benefits for migrants to the city because it means that they can quickly find work, set up their own business or join relatives or friends in their work. But there are major downsides in terms of quality of life. There is no protection for workers in the informal sector, so working conditions may be very challenging and dangerous. There is no sick pay if people become unwell and cannot work. The rapid economic development of Mexico City also means that people are forced to live in slums or squatter settlements because there is not enough affordable housing for all the people who want to come and live in the city. Many new migrants have to live in shacks on rubbish dumps or polluted waste land. Quality of life here is very low, but even in more developed squatter settlements and slums there is often no piped water, no proper sewerage system and no mains electricity. These places are dangerous to live in because of criminal gangs, and because the open sewers spread deadly diseases like typhoid and cholera.
Rapid economic development also leads to environmental problems such as air pollution and waste pollution. People's dream when they come to Mexico City is to buy a car – cars are a huge step up in quality of life because you can then live in a nicer area on the outskirts of the city and commute to a job anywhere else in the city. However, the huge increase in quality of life means millions of cars and other vehicles, creating heavy air pollution that has a highly negative impact on people's quality of life: many people in Mexico City suffer from respiratory diseases.
Poor communities do not produce much waste: it is mainly organic and all recycled one way or another. But economic development means people consume a lot more, creating a lot more waste. Mexico City generates 13 000 tonnes of waste every day. Over the years of Mexico's rapid economic development, 70 million tonnes of waste have been buried as landfill, which is now polluting Mexico's water, also affecting quality of life.
In conclusion, while economic development has led to huge increases in opportunities for people in LICs and NEEs, and raised billions out of severe rural poverty around the world, it is not possible to argue that economic development only has positive effects on quality of life. The impacts of rapid growth in cities have meant that quality of life remains very difficult for many because of the lack of adequate housing and the lack of adequate infrastructure.

129. Paper 3
1 **B** Paper 3 Section A Issue evaluation: 9-mark decision-making question
2 **B** Paper 3 Section B Fieldwork: 9-mark 'to what extent' question on reliability
3 **A** Apply knowledge and understanding to interpret, analyse and evaluate geographical information and issues to make judgements

130. Atlas and map skills
1 (a) Brazil – black (high); Kenya – dots (lower-middle); Saudi Arabia – black (high); Ukraine – dots (newly emerging)

(b) **D** Choropleth
(c) The highest income countries can be found in the continents of <u>North America and Europe in the Northern Hemisphere, where income levels are US$11 116 or more. The lowest income countries are mainly found in Africa and Asia.</u>

131. Types of map and scale
1 Most hot deserts occur close to the Tropics of Cancer and Capricorn. The greatest extent of hot desert is in <u>a belt across North Africa and the Middle East.</u>
2 (a) 140 m
(b) 300 m

132. Grid references and distances

1 (a) **C** 091923
  (b) 6 km
  (c) Telephone
  (d) 224 m
  (e) 087919

133. Cross sections and relief

1 **A** – iii; **B** – i; **C** – ii
2 The land to the east of the River Otter is <u>steep</u>. It rises to a maximum height of <u>99 m</u> above sea level. In comparison, the land to the west of the river is <u>flatter</u> and rises to a height of approximately <u>70 m</u> above sea level.
3 *See page 157 for answer.*

134. Physical and human patterns

1 (a) Alnwick has a nucleated settlement shape because <u>it is clustered around main roads and sandwiched between the A1 and the B6341, which runs from the south-west of Alnwick.</u>
  (b) *Example* Alnwick will have difficulty expanding because there is coniferous woodland to the north-west of the settlement, in GR 1713. This will need to be deforested to allow expansion. There is farmland to the east of the A1, therefore land is valuable for primary industry. The flow of the River Aln is to the north and north-east, so will inhibit development. There is high relief to the west and south-west, which is difficult to build on.

135. Human activity and OS maps

1 (a) School or infirmary
  (b) Bus, because there is evidence of a bus station
  (c) Two from: post office; pub; church.
  (d) Shilbottle is surrounded by a rural landscape. The many farms around the area help prove this. For example, South East Farm is located to the south east of Shilbottle. The map also shows <u>a lack of built-up areas – it is mainly an agricultural landscape. Transport routes are limited to roads less than 4 m wide, which supports limited rural population. Contour lines show that this is an upland area and therefore the landscape is not able to support the growth of large settlements.</u>

136. Sketch maps and annotations

1 (a) **C** B = river cliff, C = fast-flowing water, D = slow-flowing water
  (b) A river cliff is the steep-sided bank of the river which forms when <u>fast-moving water erodes the sides of the bank, causing the top of the bank to collapse into the river</u>. *Note: the emphasis of your answer should be on explanatory detail.*
2 *See page 157 for answer.*

137. Using and interpreting images

1 (a) **B** Oblique aerial
  (b) Advantage 1: It is easy to compare different land uses. *Example* Advantage 2: <u>Indicates height and density of settlements</u>. *Other options: outline of transport network is clear; photograph available for use quicker than map; provides record of the area that day.*
2 The contours and spot heights give the height of the land.

138. Graphical skills 1

1 (a) *See page 157 for answer.*
  (b) 130 – 60 = 70 per cent
  (c) Eight years (between 2000 and 2008)

139. Graphical skills 2

1 (a) *See page 157 for answer.*
  (b) 30 vehicles: 12 cars, 3 buses, 6 lorries, 4 vans, 5 motorbikes
2 (a) Population pyramid (also known as an age-structure graph or a specific form of divided bar graph)
  (b) The country shown has a high <u>birth rate: the base of the pyramid is very wide, and there are lots of children in the 0–4 age band. The top of pyramid is very narrow, indicating a high death rate.</u> *Other points: there is a youthful population – the pyramid narrows considerably above the 30–34 age band; life expectancy in men is lower than in women.*
  (c) Line graphs are used to show trends or patterns, or to see if there is a correlation between two sets of data. The traffic data cannot be shown as a line graph as it does not show a change over time.

140. Graphical skills 3

1 (a) Proportional circles/symbols
  (b) *Example* Advantage: The graphic representation makes initial comparison between data very straightforward. *Other options: easy to understand; give a strong visual impression of the data.* Disadvantage: <u>Unless figures are also given, proportional circles do not provide precise values of the data.</u> *Other options: if data are presented close together the proportional circles can overlap and make the data less clear; if two circles are close in size it is not easy to tell which is the larger and which the smaller.*
2 **A** Desire line map

141. Numbers and statistics 1

1 (a) 17.8 per cent: 1 311 050 521 ÷ 7 349 472 099 = 0.1783 × 100 = 17.8 (to 1 decimal place)
  (b) 6.5 per cent
  (c) A line graph would be the best way to represent India's population data because the data show changes over time.
2 833 087 662 ÷ 377 105 760 = <u>2.2:1</u>. This means for every 1 person living in an urban area in India <u>there are 2.2 people living in rural areas. Therefore, the ratio of rural to urban population in rural areas in India in 2011 is 2.2:1</u>.

142. Numbers and statistics 2

1 (a) 18.03 m³/s
  (b) 8.4 m³/s
  (c) The interquartile range is a measure of dispersion around the average. It omits the very extreme values.
  (d) 8.1 (Values in order: 10.7, 14.8, 17.7, 18.6, 22.6, 22.9, 23.2. Seven numbers, so median value is 4th value, lower quartile is 2nd value and upper quartile is 6th value. Interquartile range is the difference between the lower and upper quartiles.)
  (e) The discharge data could be used by authorities involved in the management of <u>river flooding</u>.

39. The cold environment ecosystem

1 (b)

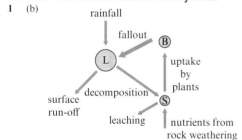

47. Erosion, transport, deposition

2

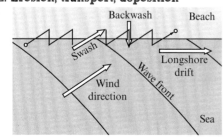

48. Erosion landforms

1 (b)

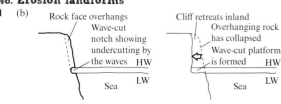

49. Deposition landforms

1 (b)

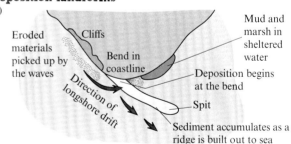

58. Deposition landforms

2 When a river is in spate or bankfull, water will spill onto the flood plain. The river will deposit the heaviest sediment at the sides of the river as energy is not great enough to carry it away from the river. This process continually repeats during flood events and will eventually form raised embankments called levees.

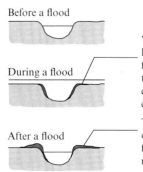

When flooding occurs, the heaviest material is deposited first due to the decrease in the river's energy. This material creates natural embankments called levees.

The smaller and finer sediment, or alluvium, is deposited further from the river because it requires less energy to carry it.

64. Glacial processes

1 (a)

freeze-thaw weathering

transposition

deposition

(b)

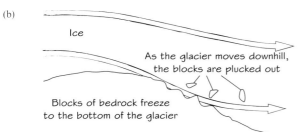

Ice

As the glacier moves downhill, the blocks are plucked out

Blocks of bedrock freeze to the bottom of the glacier

65. Erosion landforms 1

3

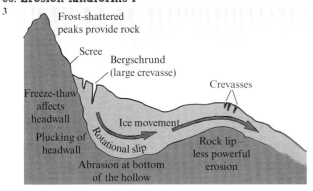

Frost-shattered peaks provide rock

Scree

Bergschrund (large crevasse)

Crevasses

Freeze-thaw affects headwall

Ice movement

Plucking of headwall

Rotational slip

Rock lip – less powerful erosion

Abrasion at bottom of the hollow

66. Erosion landforms 2

1 (a) Your diagram doesn't need to indicate the U-shape of the U-shape valley but doing it like this does make what you are labelling clearer.

truncated spur

U-shaped valley

(b) Your diagram should show interlocking spurs instead of truncated spurs. The valley should be V-shaped rather than U-shaped. Instead of the stream being a misfit stream in the glaciated valley, it should wind between its spurs.

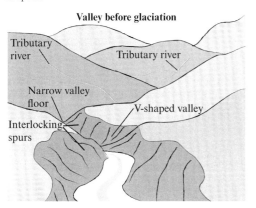

Valley before glaciation

Tributary river

Tributary river

Narrow valley floor

V-shaped valley

Interlocking spurs

133. Cross sections and relief

3

West A Top of hill B East

Height of land in metres

136. Sketch maps and annotations

2

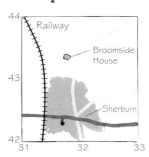

Railway

Broomside House

Sherburn

138. Graphical skills 1

1 (a)

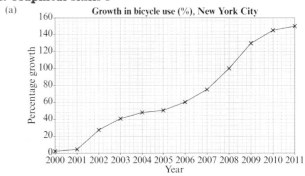

Growth in bicycle use (%), New York City

Percentage growth

Year

139. Graphical skills 2

1 (a)

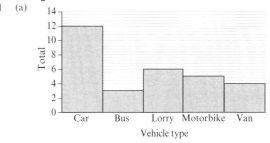

Total

Car Bus Lorry Motorbike Van

Vehicle type

Published by Pearson Education Limited, 80 Strand, London, WC2R 0RL.

www.pearsonschoolsandfecolleges.co.uk

Text © Pearson Education Limited 2017
Typeset and illustrated by Kamae Design, Oxford
Produced by Out of House Publishing
Cover illustration by Miriam Sturdee

The right of Rob Bircher to be identified as author of this work has been asserted by him in accordance with the Copyright, Designs and Patents Act 1988.

First published 2017

20 19 18
10 9 8 7 6 5 4

British Library Cataloguing in Publication Data
A catalogue record for this book is available from the British Library

ISBN 978 1 292 13131 3

Acknowledgements
Content written by Anne-Marie Grant, David Holmes and Andrea Wood is included.

The author and publisher would like to thank the following individuals and organisations for permission to reproduce copyright material:

Photographs
(Key: b-bottom; c-centre; l-left; r-right; t-top)

123RF.com: kessudap 117; **Alamy Stock Photo:** Arctic Images 118, Ashley Cooper 39, 89, Dorothy Alexander 74, Eye Candy Images 3 69, Ian G Dagnall 123r, Jeff Morgan 12 122, Kevin Britland 50, Mauritius images GmbH 41, Mike Greenslade 137, Nick Lylak 84, Pictorial Press Ltd 67, Pink Sun Media 123l, Richard Franklin 70, Universal Images Group North America LLC 28, Werli Francois 112, Zach Holmes 1; **Getty Images:** Anadolu Agency 116, Eric Lafforgue / Art in All of Us 108, Geography Photos 51, Jim Reed 14, Keren Su 30, Marko Georgiev 13, Robin Smith 43; **Reuters:** Ricardo Moraes 119; **Science Photo Library Ltd:** US Geological Survey 7; **Shutterstock. com:** aricvyhmeister 61, Dr Morley Read 27, Ingus Kruklitis 34, JaySi 64, 157, Mel Thompson 66, 157

All other images © Pearson Education

Figures
Page 18 British Antarctic Survey; page 35 reprinted with permission of International Renewable Energy Agency (IRENA). Retrieved from http://www.mdpi.com/2073-4441/6/5/1134/htm#B11-water-06-; page 101 used with permission of Ernst & Young; page 105 map © Guardian News & Media Ltd 2017.

Maps
Pages 49, 132, 134, 136, 137 Ordnance Survey maps © Crown copyright 2016, OS 100030901 and supplied by courtesy of Maps International; pages 59, 68, 82 maps © Crown Copyright 2015. All rights reserved. Licence Number 100031961 courtesy of National Map Centre.

Text
Page 127 Storm Desmond reprinted with permission of Wales online. Retrieved from http://www.walesonline.co.uk/news/wales-news/storm-desmond-pictures-show-devastating-10555403.

Note from the publisher
Pearson has robust editorial processes, including answer and fact checks, to ensure the accuracy of the content in this publication, and every effort is made to ensure this publication is free of errors. We are, however, only human, and occasionally errors do occur. Pearson is not liable for any misunderstandings that arise as a result of errors in this publication, but it is our priority to ensure that the content is accurate. If you spot an error, please do contact us at resourcescorrections@pearson.com so we can make sure it is corrected.